River of Lost Dreams

River of Lost Dreams

Navigation on the Rio Grande

by Pat Kelley

University of Nebraska Press: Lincoln and London

The paper in this book meets the
minimum requirements of American National Standard for Information Sciences – Permanence of
Paper for Printed Library Materials,
ANSI Z39.48–1984.

Library of Congress Cataloging-
in-Publication Data
Kelley, Pat, 1928 –
River of lost dreams.
Bibliography: p.
Includes index.
1. Rio Grande—Description and
travel.   2. Rio Grande – Navigation.   3. Rio Grande Valley –
History.   I. Title.
F392.R5K45   1986   976.4'4
86-4340   ISBN 0-8032-2712-4
(alkaline paper)

To Les Gower, a Tennesseean transplant-
ed to Texas some twenty years ago.
So Texan has Les become that in 1979
he was commissioned an admiral in the
Texas Navy by Acting Governor Raul
Longoria of Edinburg. As director of
University Libraries and the Learning Resource Center at Pan American University, he has created a rare documents
and special collection division and has
secured for the library the status of se-
lective documents depository. Together,
these two accomplishments have made
the university a significant resource for
scholars who study southern Texas and
northern Mexico.

Les deserves much of the credit for
this volume. His encouragement, prod-
ding, and collections saw it through its
formative stage, and his interest encouraged its completion. He is an explorer, a
visionary, a doer. South Texas and northern Mexico need more people like him.

Contents

Maps

Illustrations

Preface

In North America two river systems have had an overwhelming influence on events: the Mississippi and the Rio Grande, or Bravo del Norte. Folklorists, singers, historians, and novelists have presented the Mississippi in all of its many contours. Mike Fink and Huck Finn and Abe Lincoln coursed its path through the center of the nation. The "Big Muddy" was the highway by which jazz and ragtime found their way into the national language. Today it still provides the means for farms and factories of the Midwest and South to deliver their products to market; its tributaries power the bulk of the nation. The Mississippi is America.

But what of the Rio Grande? There was a time when the Great River seemed destined to challenge the Mississippi as a highway of commerce and epic folklore. The river drew men and nations as a magnet attracts iron filings; it was capable of floating ships and commerce for a thousand miles. And there was a time when it signified destiny, gripped the national consciousness, and created a war.

That river is not at all the river that flows tranquilly through the Texas-Mexican subdesert today. Keelboats and steamboats no longer wind their crooked way up and down, seeking cargo and carrying trade goods. Some things happened along the way to change all that. This book is about those things.

I first got infected with an interest in navigation on the Rio Grande while working on a television documentary about Nuevo Dolores, an abandoned village on the ranch of the late Juan E. Martínez a few miles south of Laredo. The site was originally occupied in 1859 (although one house dates from earlier times) after Don Cosme Martínez bought the site from heirs of the original grantee. It remained occupied until the 1930s, when most of its few remaining inhabitants moved to Laredo. A considerable body of folklore has grown up around the town.

An old man living on the Mercurio Martínez ranch, not far from Nuevo

Dolores, told of his youth in the town, of how a steamboat coming down-river from Laredo had grounded on a double reef, of how the young men of the town had helped free her, and of the fiesta and dance held on her decks that night.

Folklore, the scholars told me. It was not. The incident really happened —not quite the way the old man remembered it, but it happened. From that point on, I was captured by the river.

Initially, I had to define the limits of navigation on the river, as well as commercial and military use of them. I discovered that commercial use never approximated the limits and that the military abandoned the river altogether. Why? Usually railroads led to the decline of navigation on west-ern rivers; but on the Rio Grande, railroads had little influence, although their presence did stifle the early beginnings of navigation on the upper river. As I explored the problem, I discovered that Mexican trade had dic-tated the commercial limits of navigation and that a true river trade never developed. The military abandoned the river because a desire for commer-cial monopoly led to the corruption of the military, resulting in its failure to press for an open river. (An open river would have precluded monopoly and meant the expansion of competition.)

If river navigation—by flatboat, keelboat, or steamboat—is to be suc-cessful, it requires three conditions: a populated, productive region up-river with goods to sell and a need for others' goods; a populated, produc-tive region downriver that needs upriver goods and has goods to trade; and a port at or near the mouth to serve as a terminal and commercial center for trade all along the river. The Rio Grande potentially had all those things. When railroads finally became a factor in the Mexican trade, navi-gation on the river should actually have expanded. Why, then, did it de-cline instead of increasing? First, the population and industry requisite to a river trade was only beginning to assert itself. Second, and more impor-tant, the river channel was undergoing radical change brought about by massive irrigation projects in the upper reaches of the river.

Factors other than economic issues also entered into the Rio Grande's failure to progress as a navigable stream. Population and industry were stunted by the effects of climate, the vagaries of policies, and the shifting currents of national objectives as they affected river use.

Such issues formed the bases for my examination of the Rio Grande as a carrier of commerce and trade. In order to validate each base, I had to maintain geographical, historical, and biographical perspective. If I wrote of the Rio Grande during its historical periods, I had to keep within the context of each period. If I investigated the economics of navigation, I had to relate those economics to the Great River.

In the course of this study, I consulted Spanish, Mexican, British, Texan, and American archives; studied letters and diaries; and perused indexes and bibliographies, books and articles, folklore and oral history. Through them, *River of Lost Dreams* examines navigation on the Rio Grande from that unknown Laredoan who took a flatboat downriver to Reynosa to trade for salt, to the attempt of W. W. Follett—who built a launch but had a propeller put on her instead of a paddlewheel—to navigate a once-great river that had become shallow and treacherous. In between, a history develops —one that is almost Gothic in its unfolding.

This book would not have been possible without the cooperation and assistance of many scholars, archivists, and friends. There is really no way to thank them or give them the plaudits they deserve. So, rather than risk not mentioning one or two whose contributions were meritorious, let me say that I have deeply appreciated all their efforts.

I must, however, mention two whose devotion to learning has impressed me deeply. Robert B. Matchette of the Navy and Old Army Archives assisted far beyond the call of duty. Without his aid and interest, much of the material published here for the first time would have remained unpublished. Sylvia Kelley, my wife and a gifted grammarian, had the patience to put up with the research and writing, to contribute ideas and time, and to do the final proofreading with skill and competence.

Genesis

Chapter 1

Rivers once meant industrial, commercial, and communicative potency. They powered industrial complexes, served as transportation highways, and made rapid, safe communication possible. Rivers and their interconnecting canals were the sources of a nation's strength. When men and nations viewed great rivers in those centuries, they dreamed of these things and had visions that encompassed personal or national glory.

The Rio Bravo—the Brave, Wild River, sometimes called Grande del Norte—was such a river. It was a powerful, pulsating wilderness river, swelling with a rush in the spring as the snowpack of the Rocky Mountains began its melt in southern Colorado and upper New Mexico. It spurted with a rush, then the flood slowed down, keeping the river in high water until autumn freezes and winter snows slowed it. Then, as now, the river flowed almost due south more than six hundred miles to Paso del Norte, passing its waters on to the crops of agricultural Indians in upper New Mexico and Chihuahua. There the Great River of the North turned to the southeast for 292 miles before the Conchos, its first major tributary, entered from the south; the Rio Grande turned to the northeast a few miles below the Conchos, forming the Big Bend. From the Conchos through the Big Bend the river flowed for 270 miles before turning to the east. Then it traveled some forty miles before the Pecos entered from the northwest; 41 miles further, the Devil's River joined the Rio del Norte from the same direction. The river then turned to the south-southeast for another 275 miles, and the Rio Salado entered from the southwest; 38 miles further the Alamo came in from the Mexican mountains, and the river made an abrupt turn to the east. The last major tributary, the San Juan, came into the Rio Grande 21 miles down. It, too, flowed from the southwest. After another 70 miles, the river—unlike today's tamed Rio Grande—split into three channels and flowed through semisubmerged lands. It twisted and turned, as it still does, seemingly unable to make up its mind about its destination. One channel flowed off to the northeast and made its brackish way to Laguna Madre; another meandered into small lakes and resacas. The southernmost, main channel continued for 170 miles (about seventy miles by land) to the Gulf of Mexico.[1]

And always the river was—and is—in a perpetual state of drought or semidrought. The lands it drains are desert lands, or almost so. Its replenishing water comes from the Rocky Mountains and from the mountains of Mexico. Nature makes no effort along its course to assist with either rainfall or dependable tributaries. Yet, despite its arid antecedent basin and all of its twisting and turning in the lower reaches, the Rio Grande was, until after the Mexican War, a broad, deep river from the Gulf to about the Rio Alamo. It was never less than 200 yards wide (mostly two or three times that wide), and so deep that even in times of drought it could not be forded below the San Juan.

From the San Juan, upriver navigators found the channel clear of obstacles until just above the entrance of the Rio Salado. An island with a shoal of sand and gravel blocked a deep channel on one side, and the other channel, though deep enough, was clogged with shafts of rock sticking straight up from the bottom, creating problems on either side in low water. Even so, boats with a draft of no more than two and a half feet could make passage in middle or high water. The channel, though bordered by reefs and rocks, was then relatively clear of any but minor shoals or reefs until 15 miles below El Paso de Jacinto—the site of Laredo, some 377 miles from the Gulf. There, twin reefs appeared to block further passage, except in high water. A channel did exist, though. One reef ran out from the west bank of the river but ended before reaching the eastern shore; the other jutted out from the east bank but stopped short before abutting the other side. The reefs formed a sinuous channel that had to be navigated with care and caution.

From the twin reefs to the falls of the Rio Grande, about a hundred more miles, the river was clear. There, the river drops more than two hundred feet in a span of four miles, flowing through many small islands with a rushing torrent and spilling over what appear to be natural dams offering no channel; but at the time of early exploration there was one, blocked by but a single reef. Once past the falls, the river was open to the Devil's River—575 miles from the Gulf of Mexico. There was sharp disagreement as to whether the navigability of the river ended at the Devil's River or at the Pecos. There, most agreed, the limits of steamboat navigation had been reached, although a few keelboats had actually made their way to within 35 miles of the Rio Conchos—926 miles upriver from the mouth. This was the ultimate limit of navigation from the Gulf of Mexico; after a brief stretch of rocks, ledges, and rapids, the river was again navigable from a site 147 miles below El Paso upriver to the city by steamboats of 100 to 150 tons, and perhaps beyond for smaller craft.[2]

European exploration and navigation of the Rio Grande was contemporary with Cortez's conquest of Mexico. Alonso Alvarez de Pineda, sailing under a commission from Francisco Garay, governor of Jamaica, skirted and mapped the coast of the Gulf of Mexico from the tip of Florida westward. As he sailed down the western coast, he sighted a long, thin, sandy barrier island. His men landed at the southern tip of it and erected a marker.[3] His ships then rounded the tip of a smaller island just south of the first landing, made it over a bar, and sailed up a palm-lined stream. "Rio de las Palmas," they called it. The local Indians seemed friendly. Pineda noted these things, retraced his way to the Gulf, and sailed on.

Almost immediately, attempts at settlement began. All failed, primarily because the Spanish incurred the enmity of the local Indians by mistreating them. The early Spanish settlers might have overcome the Indian problem, however, but for one thing. Cortez, far to the south, was pillaging the civilized tribes of Mexico, looting gold and silver and power. The harassed Spaniards on the River of Palms fled south. Gold was worth sacrifice. There was no gold on the river.[4]

The Spanish spread north and west from Veracruz, conquering and enslaving all the way. Mexico was subdued, all but a womb-shaped region stretching from the northern limits of Veracruz up the coast. It was bordered on the west by mountains, the Sierra Gorda. Both the coastal Indians and their mountain-dwelling counterparts were difficult to conquer. There was no ready gold or silver in the region. Conquest was not worth the effort. The Seno Mexicano (Mexican Womb) was left to itself as settlement

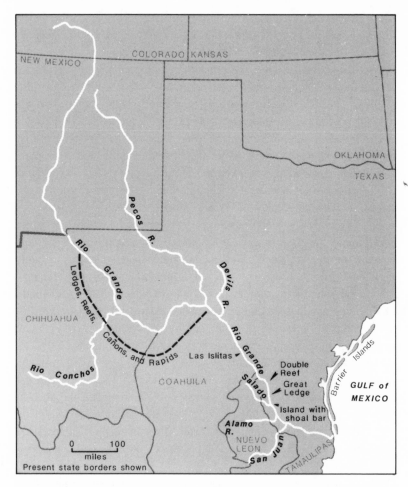

The Wilderness Rio Grande

spread slowly along its western border. Eventually that settlement reached the Rio Grande, 461 miles upriver from the aborted sixteenth-century settlement on the Rio de las Palmas. In 1699 a mission was established there, at San Juan Bautista, and two years later a presidio of soldiers was based nearby to protect it. Presidio del Rio Grande was to have an important role in the future history of the river, for from it *entradas* set out, seeking French interlopers and exploring the country to the north and east, finally conquering the northern portion of the Seno.

By 1743 much of northern Mexico west of the Seno was partially settled. Productive mines were producing gold and silver; mission farms for the Indians and haciendas for the Spanish were established. The Indians of the Seno periodically raided and pillaged the Spanish and generally treated them as badly as the Spanish had treated them. The situation became intolerable. If the missions, the haciendas, and the towns were to be protected, if the produce of the mines was to be realized, the Seno had to be conquered.

The Spanish Crown had other problems with the Seno, too. The French were claiming the Rio Grande as the western and southern boundary of Louisiana; it appeared that the English might be contemplating an attempt to seize the unconquered region. In addition, the Seno Indians were troublesome and in need of Christianizing. These concerns were transmitted to the viceroy in Mexico City. The *audiencio* decided to conquer and settle the Seno Mexicano, naming the future province Nuevo Santander and giving its conqueror broad powers to settle and govern it. After a long, deliberate examination of competing plans for conquest and settlement, José de Escandón was awarded the task. At last, after more than two centuries, the Seno was to be tamed, and the Rio Grande would flow through settled, populated lands.[5]

The conquest proved amazingly simple; the Indians were surprisingly tranquil, even helping Escandón find the ideal rendezvous point for the seven columns of troops that converged on the Seno in the winter of 1747. There was no dearth of settlers, either. Nobleman or commoner, each wanted land for expanding flocks and herds or land for himself and his heirs. By 1755 on the Rio Grande, towns or villas had been founded at Reynosa (on the south bank), at Camargo, Mier, and Revilla—each on a stream tributary to the Rio Grande and only a short distance from its south or west bank. Communities were also established on the east bank at Hacienda de Dolores and at Laredo.

In 1757 the viceroy directed a general inspection of the new province. Don José Tienda de Cuervo was named inspector-general; he was to find the answers to a series of questions concerning the province's towns and villas, rivers, ports (to the Spanish, *port* meant the mouth of a river, not a trading center), and commerce. Tienda de Cuervo wrote his report in true bureaucratic fashion, answering the proffered questions in detail where possible. There was little detail, however, when he wrote of the Rio Grande: "The Rio Grande or Bravo del Norte . . . passes by the presidio San Juan Bautista and enters the colony at Laredo. . . . Near the coast it divides into three branches, one of which forms many lakes, and the other two flow into the sea. Small boats may navigate in the mouth of the Rio Grande del Norte, according to information that I have been able to acquire."[6]

Tienda de Cuervo's inspection revealed the problems of settlers in the arid lands of the Rio Grande.[7] At Laredo, there was almost no farming, the banks of the river being too high to permit irrigation. Attempts at farming the bottomland were futile: spring floods washed out the labor put into them. Cattle ranching was the primary industry, and salt was acquired forty leagues to the north by mule trains. Citizens went regularly to mine the salt, which was of inferior quality to that found north of the river across from Reynosa.

Reynosa had plenty of salt of exceedingly good quality and furnished it to all the river towns except Laredo. Mule trains were the means of carting it back to the towns, there not being enough timber to build boats. There was some farming at Revilla, Mier, and Camargo, as well as Reynosa, but the difficulty of arranging irrigation ditches severely restricted production. The principal production of all the towns and villas was the result of stock-raising.

There was a ferry at Hacienda de Dolores—a good one, too. Although Tienda de Cuervo referred to the ferry as consisting of *canoas,* it was more than that. One user of it described the boat that he crossed in as one "with a fine sail."[8] Evidently Captain Borrego, owner of the hacienda, had at least one flatboat equipped with a stern sail. It would not be the last such on the Rio Grande.

Sometime after the inspection, a citizen of Laredo procured a flatboat. He used it to go downriver to Reynosa, where he traded for that town's superior salt.[9] The river was getting used.

In 1787, several years after the death of Escandón, Friar Vicente Santa María published a history of the province.[10] Santa María was a scholar dedicated to the saving of souls and, later, to the freedom of Mexico. Whether or not the friar ever personally viewed the Rio Grande is unclear, although Alejandro Prieto, the definitive historian of the region, refers to him as the "traveller Santa María."[11] Prieto quotes him verbatim in lieu of rewriting his geographical descriptions. What is clear is that Santa María was a well-read scholar, that he was apparently aware of attempts to the north to "canalize" the Ohio valley with the settled regions of the United States,[12] and that he knew the importance of the Mississippi to Louisiana and the United States. As later events proved, he was also aware of the American Declaration of Independence, and he subscribed wholeheartedly to its principles.

In commenting on the geography of Nuevo Santander, Santa María lists five principal rivers and describes them in detail. The fourth principal river of the colony was the "Rio Bravo, or Grande del Norte."

[It is] among the rivers of primary greatness in all America, and it is the greatest river west of the Mississippi for its circumstances and utility. . . . It flows through and enriches all the province of New Mexico, the province of Coahuila, and by the pass called Jacinto where it enters the colony. . . .

Its major floods always begin in the Spring, suddenly, with the melting of the heavy snows which fall during the frigid winter at its headwaters. It is then made navigable through all the spaces of the colony for medium-sized boats and perhaps farther—into the provinces of Coahuila and New Mexico.[13]

Santa María goes on to give an accurate description of obstacles to navigation, including reefs, shallows, and the falls of the Rio Grande. He concludes this particular examination by saying, "This river, without doubt, is one of the most interesting objects of just attention, not only to the colony but to all those interior provinces contiguous to it or near it. It is like the networks of the Mississippi which serve a successful colony . . . and its environs."

His concluding sentence indicates the power of the Rio Grande. "One can say without equivocation that the Rio Bravo or Grande del Norte can become as the Mississippi has become to Louisiana."

Santa María was aware of the flatboat trade between Laredo and Reynosa, or he would not have pronounced the river navigable so forcefully (elsewhere in his work he footnotes questionable claims); he may have been aware of continuing complaints of a contraband tobacco trade being conducted from Laredo, a trade more easily carried on by flatboat downriver than by any other method. In fact, contraband tobacco may have been the medium of trade for salt.[14]

Santa María was not aware, however, of any upriver navigation from the Gulf of Mexico. At another point in the work he says that he has heard of no upriver navigation from the seas. "I shall bring attention," he writes, "to any attempt by any boats to navigate upriver."[15] At this time in the river's history, the Laredo flatboat trade was all that existed. The lack of a port at the mouth of the river negated any other. For some reason, the Spanish were extremely jealous of trade. The only port to which foreign traders had legal access was Veracruz. All foreign goods brought into New Spain had to come by that port, as well as all Mexican goods ticketed for export. Veracruz had a choking monopoly on trade. The few other ports that existed were only for coastal shipping—from Veracruz, if foreign goods were involved. There was simply no incentive for Spanish captains to take their ships up the Rio Grande. The effort would reap no profit.

Not all of Spanish officialdom concurred with the Crown's monopolistic trade theory. Strangely, it was the type of settler Escandón had brought to the Rio Grande who encouraged Spanish officials to attempt to get an open port at the mouth of the Rio Grande.

Although the Indians had been tranquil during the period from 1747 to 1757, their peaceful repose was not to last. By 1790 many local tribes had become restless because they had been mistreated at missions, and the Comanches were beginning to conduct raids into the lower Rio Grande country. At Hacienda de Dolores, Captain Borrego organized a "flying squadron" of twelve men whose only duty was to patrol and to find and ward off attacking war parties.[16] At Laredo, one Comanche raid succeeded in taking the powder house and looting it of guns and gunpowder.[17] The raids were menacing, and they threatened to overwhelm the stock-raising citizens of the Rio Grande. The situation became so serious that the Crown instructed the viceroy to have an inspection made to discover how to pacify the Indians and make life a little more bearable for the northern provinces.

Felix Calleja del Rey was chosen to make the inspection. Calleja proved to be less of a bureaucrat and more of a dreamer than any of his predecessors. His dreams did not encompass Mexican independence, as Santa María's did. They were directed more at making the settlements on the Rio Grande, and the contiguous provinces, secure for the Spanish Crown. Calleja was a dedicated Royalist who, fifteen years after his inspection of Nuevo Santander, would put down the rebellion of Padre Hidalgo and be rewarded with a title: Count of Calderon. In 1813 he would be made viceroy with the expectation that he could successfully put down the many sporadic, guerrilla-like rebellions demanding Mexican independence. But all that was in the future. In 1795 there was a need to pacify the Indians of the northern provinces. Calleja was to recommend the means.

He was a professional soldier who had come to New Spain in 1789 as a captain in an infantry regiment and immediately distinguished himself in the Indian struggles of the interior provinces. The following year he was made lieutenant colonel and commandant of the militia of the Cavalry of the Frontiers of the Sierra Gorda. He was stationed in San Luis Potosí when he received orders to make an inspection of the colony of Nuevo Santander as well as other troubled interior provinces. In his instructions, almost as an afterthought, he was told to investigate the economic situation and make recommendations for its improvement. It was those recommendations that revealed both his vision and his philosophy.[18]

Colonel Calleja found an appalling situation. Indians were threatening the very existence of the colony. Any semblance of trade had vanished. The hardy Spanish pioneers were near annihilation. Calleja reported all of the problems, but the one that bothered him most was economic and social. The economic problems, he discovered, were not to be blamed on Indian war parties, but rather on stock-raising practices. He wrote: "The haciendas and ranches are segments of land without limits nor landmarks in which each settler has his stock. He changes his stock when he wishes, and moves the hacienda to another location. Few of the settlers have fixed boundaries, though each was assigned his own. In the disorder to which all contribute, this undeterminate [*sic*] right of property has been established or at most accepted as a workable system."

It is evident that Calleja did not appreciate the necessities of open range in the pre–barbed wire era. The hardy Spanish ranchers and vaqueros were establishing a tradition that would give western folklore a new, vital source of material. What concerned Calleja was the economic and social effect that this lack of respect for fixed boundaries had on the population. "Their occupations are limited all year to branding," he wrote. "Commerce is purely barter among the people or with peddlers, with whom they exchange mules for goods." This economic chaos did not distress the able inspector nearly as much as did the resultant social attitudes that such self-reliance bred. Indeed, the ranchers and citizens of the Rio Grande had become somewhat westernized by their lonely, independent existence. "In character and customs, the people are lazy, dissipated, with relative luxury in their arms, dress, and horses, without courage, captious, and sarcastic murmurers, all stemming from the fact that the population of this province was formed from among the vagabonds and malefactors of the others."

Calleja pondered long and hard over possible solutions to the problems revealed by his inspection. The Indian problem, he felt, could be overcome. But what of the economic and social disorder that he found in Nuevo Santander? Finally, the visionary in him overcame the soldier. He prefaced his recommendations by pointing out that the right kind of new settler would have a proper influence on those already there, that the desired settler could be induced to come to the province only if trade and commerce were begun by opening a port—if only auxiliary to Veracruz— at the mouth of the Rio Grande. Then he said, "[The] Rio Grande seems to be navigable to Laredo, 100 leagues distant from the sea and very close to the four provinces [of Coahuila, Nuevo Santander, Nuevo Leon, and Texas]. . . . If [there] were to be made an auxiliary free port, it seems to me it would be the channel to abundant peopling and prosperity of the four provinces. . . . The different and exquisite woods, the skins of deer, buffalo, and beaver, and even pearls, would then become items of no little value."

Calleja—soldier, Royalist, inspector of Nuevo Santander and the inte-

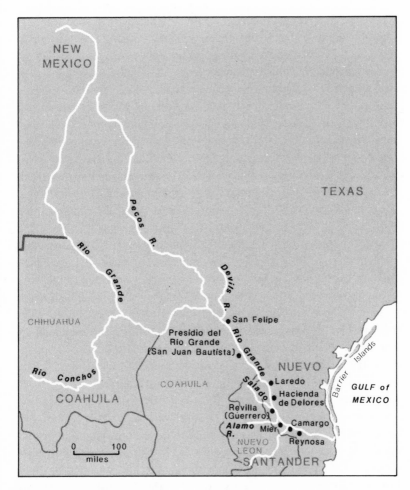

Settlement on the Lower River

rior provinces—seized upon the Rio Grande as the answer to the problems he found. Navigable to Laredo, it could provide the wherewithal to satisfy the economic needs of the provinces and lead to their economic—and social—improvement. He saw the Rio Grande as a second Mississippi, providing a commerce that would enrich both the provinces and the

Crown. Calleja's recommendations for the improvement of economic and social conditions in Nuevo Santander, and the Rio Grande country in particular, had to wait for action. New Spain underwent a lengthy, chaotic period of transition leading to the emergence of an independent and sovereign Mexico. The American Revolution had not been lost on Mexican citizens. In 1809 a plot to begin the movement for Spanish expulsion was prematurely disclosed. Fr. Vicente Santa María, among others, was executed. A year later, Padre Hidalgo rang the bell and shouted the *grito*. His tattered forces were defeated at Calderon by Calleja. But the cry for a free Mexico would not go away. Mexican patriots banded together throughout New Spain; guerrilla fighters picked up the banner of independence. Organized filibustering expeditions from the United States and Europe, aided and created by Mexican patriots, assaulted the Spanish.

The Rio Grande did not escape the feverish turmoil that accompanied the fight for independence. When Padre Hidalgo shouted the cry of freedom, the Gutiérrez de Lara brothers of Revilla heard and acted. In the three years following the defeat of Hidalgo, Bernardo led an insurgent action north of the Rio Grande, visited Washington, D.C. (as an accredited agent of the revolution), and co-led an expedition that seized Texas and, but for dissension among its leaders, might have wrested that province from the Spanish. (The brothers also printed pamphlets calling for freedom on the American model—and prudently had them distributed by Indians.)

While the Gutiérrez de Lara brothers and others were waging the fight for independence, Napoleon was overthrown and the Bourbon king of Spain regained his throne. One of his first acts was to repudiate the liberal constitution of 1812. A disenchanted young Spanish aristocrat and republican, Francisco Xavier Mina, was determined to go to Mexico and help free that hapless possession from royal tyranny. In 1816 he arrived in the United States, procured some volunteers, stocked his ships, and sailed on. Following some misadventures, his force landed at Soto la Marina. After a few initial successes, Mina's expedition failed, and he was captured and executed.

His expedition's importance to the Rio Grande was enormous, for among the American volunteers was an idealistic young Virginia-born, Kentucky-raised Louisiana citizen and officer of the militia named John

Davis Bradburn.[19] That was in 1817. By the time of Mexican independence, he had fought with Vicente Guerrero, accepted Spanish amnesty (with the apparent blessing of Guerrero), assisted Augustín Iturbide, and joined a cadre of officers, Mexican and foreign, who formed the base of the Mexican military after independence.

Mexican politics following the expulsion of the Spanish became a confused tapestry of diametrically opposed ideals. The conflict between centralism and federalism was to curse the nation for more than fifty years, lie dormant, then rear its head again in the revolution of 1910. Briefly, the Centralists were those who believed in a strong, overpowering central government, with the nation subject to it; the Federalists believed in states' rights and a government almost subservient to the states. The struggle for ascendancy led to internecine warfare that strangled the Mexican economy. Mexican independence did not free the Rio Grande for exploitation; it held the river in a bondage created by political instability and commercial collapse. It did not seem that Mexico—and the Rio Grande—would suffer so in the beginning.

After the Spanish were toppled, a constitutional monarchy was created. Almost immediately, Iturbide, who had formulated the Plan de Iguala—which led to independence by unifying liberals, conservatives, and Mexican Royalists—seized the throne as Emperor Augustín I. Although his rule was short-lived, two events important to the Rio Grande occurred. Stephen F. Austin began bringing three hundred families to settle along the Brazos River in Texas, and the eyes of visionaries began again to examine the Great River.

One of those visionaries was Teodoro Ortiz y Ayala. In 1822 he published *Resumen de la estadística del imperio mexicano (Statistical Summary of the Mexican Empire)*, which laid out the resources of Mexico, the ways to develop them, and some warnings to the government about politics. His political prognostications were uncannily correct, as the next fifty-three years of Mexican history proved. His enthusiastic economic predictions came to naught. The very chaos that he warned the nation of prevented that. In the geographic section, Ortiz y Ayala noted that the Rio Grande offered the means by which to secure the northern provinces and, with the Colorado, make California safe from American expansionism.[20]

He also pointed out the external dangers to the new nation that lurked in the background. In addition to the United States, he wrote, England and Russia coveted Mexican lands. He urged that Texas be settled (not by *norteamericanos,* but by Mexicans, Irish Catholics, and others who were not interested in national expansion), the Tehuantepec settled, and California developed so that the schemes of those nations could be thwarted. The key to securing the northern provinces and California was a developed and navigable Rio Grande.

Ortiz y Ayala was much more than a writer and a prophet. He was a man of action. He proposed to settle ten thousand families from Ireland and the Canary Islands in Texas; when Congress tabled that proposal until a general colonization law was passed, he turned his attention elsewhere. He established five towns in the Tehuantepec before turning his attention to Texas once more. In 1832 he was appointed colonial administrator for Texas, and he crossed the Rio Grande.[21]

Before leaving for Texas, Ortiz y Ayala published his *Ideario mexicano (Mexican Schematta),* in which he repeated, in extremely strong terms, the necessity of protecting California and Texas from the United States. By 1832, however, he had come to realize that there was another threat to the northern provinces: Indians.

The young patriot exhorted his nation to settle the area from Texas to the Californias with dependable natives. The government should change its Indian policy, he wrote, so that the savage tribes could become civilized and friendly to Mexico. Then, as agriculturalists, they would protect the upper Rio Grande–Rio Colorado line to the Californias. In order for this to come about, the Rio Grande would have to become the transportation and communication line.[22]

Iturbide's excesses led to his overthrow and expulsion in 1823. A new federal constitution, based on that of the United States, was drawn up and ratified. It stripped the Centralists of power and placed that power in the states. One of the early acts of the new federal congress was to call for an Atlantic-Pacific communication within the limits of the Mexican republic. The decree of November 4, 1824, passed at the urging of Ortiz y Ayala, among others, ordered the government to call for proposals to connect the Atlantic and Pacific in the Tehuantepec, to set specifications for such a project and canal, and, in Article Three, to report to the Congress the best proposal made. Attention was then given to Mexican internal communication. Article Four called for proposals to open several rivers to navigation, among them the Rio Bravo del Norte.[23]

The Rio Grande was to experience the first serious attempt to open it to navigation.

Navigators

Chapter 2

Although Mexico had at least ten governments in the first ten years of its independence,[1] the period 1824–28 was stable. The Federalists controlled Congress, the presidency, and the states. It seemed as though political anarchy and economic chaos could end. Matamoros (Congregación de Refugio before independence), a small settlement fifty-five miles upriver from the Rio Grande's entrance to the Gulf, began to prosper.

After Pineda had coasted down what is today South Padre Island, he rounded a smaller island to the south in order to enter the Rio Grande. The smaller island came to be known as Brazos Island, and the passageway between the two, El Paso de Los Brazos de Santiago. A ship could slip through the pass and find an anchorage safe from the Gulf's hard-blowing trade winds and storms, but not from hurricanes. Water over the bar varied in depth from eleven feet at the entrance to around seven and a half feet some distance in, then deepened to about twenty feet at the anchorage inside the island. If a boat's draft was too deep, goods could be lightered to Point Isabel, loaded in wagons, and hauled overland. If overland transportation was not desirable, cargo could be loaded directly onto shallow draft vessels for shipment directly to Boca del Rio (the mouth of the river), over the shallow bar of the Rio Grande, and upriver. Regardless of the method chosen, most goods were then smuggled into interior Nuevo Santander (renamed Tamaulipas after independence). Quite a few traders and others who specialized in contraband goods—Jean Lafitte among them— used this method of enriching themselves and their Mexican counterparts. The contraband trade did not amount to much, though, nor did Congregación de Refugio, despite having been named an open port by Augustín I. In 1823, however, the settlement's fortunes suddenly improved. A Texas rancher, Martín de León, and Ramon LaFon, a reputed smuggler and pirate, joined forces to take a shipload of goods to Brazos Santiago and smuggle it into Tamaulipas. The venture was far more profitable than they had expected.[2]

Word of the successful speculative venture reverberated through American trade centers and eventually in Europe. Interior northern Mexico, wracked by the struggles for independence, burgeoned with produce to sell and had an appetite for goods long denied. Traders with overloaded mule trains set out from interior Tamaulipas, Nuevo Leon, and Coahuila. The trains from the latter two states moved generally through Monterrey, eastward to Mier and Camargo, and down the river road to Matamoros. There goods were traded and taken to Brazos de Santiago; sometimes lighter-draft ocean vessels sneaked over the bar of the river in high water and made the trip up to Matamoros, then back again.

Part of Calleja's vision was coming to pass. Within the twenty years following the de León–LaFon trading escapade, the new port attained a population in excess of seven thousand, many of them businessmen from the trading nations of the world. Until 1837, however, most of the international trade was with the United States. It was after 1837 that great, booming growth took place, probably because from 1830 to 1837, ships were forbidden to sail upriver to Matamoros (on the pretext that this would prevent smuggling). Then, with the idea that smuggling could be reduced, ships were once again allowed upriver. The riverfront and the Camargo road became lined with warehouses.

By 1828 Matamoros was an established port, handling cargoes that came overland from Point Isabel or upriver from Boca del Rio. The Rio Grande, however, was little used. Steam navigation had not yet reached the Great River. Eighteen twenty-eight was a pivotal year for the Rio Grande, even though political unrest in Mexico City resulted in three governments. Congress attempted to overthrow the election that year in order to perpetuate liberal federalism, and the conservative Centralists successfully overthrew both the election and Congress. General Anastasio Bustamante, commandant at Laredo, established himself as the dictator of Mexico; those who were loyal to him were rewarded. Among the army officers loyal to centralism was Colonel Juan Davis Bradburn.

Colonel Bradburn, as recompense for his long and meritorious service in the cause of Mexican independence, was given a virtual sinecure in 1824. Feeling that his days as a professional soldier were over, he married into a wealthy Mexican family and began casting about for a career that would bring him additional riches. In the process he met Stephen McL. Staples, whose family had a commission house in London and had established a branch in Mexico.[3] Staples, well versed in both surveying and topographical engineering, was, like Bradburn, looking for a way to establish his own fortune. The two became close friends and companions.

The decree of November 4, 1824, led them to attempt to open the Rio Grande to navigation as their means to fortune. Thus they became the first steam navigators of the Rio Grande.[4] Their vessel was not intended for trade (though some thought that it was), but rather to explore the limits of navigability. They also got together delegates from Tamaulipas, Nuevo Leon, Coahuila and Texas, and Chihuahua to secure from them common agreement for concessions on the Rio Grande as it passed through their dominions. Although Nuevo Leon had virtually no river channel within its boundaries, the state was glad to take part in the meeting, which was held in Monterrey early in 1828.

The newspaper *Espíritu Público* carried the story. The delegates (all either deputies or senators back home) agreed to press their respective states to grant concessions that would give Bradburn and Staples a fifteen-year monopoly for steamboats or horse-drawn vessels on the river in each state. In addition, the proposed concession gave them the right to settle ungranted lands, take timber, call upon each state for troops to protect against Indians, and transfer the concession; it also assured that no further taxes or regulations pertaining to navigation would affect them. The partners were given two years to get their project under way.[5]

Chihuahua granted the concession on March 18, 1828;[6] Coahuila and Texas acted the following month, on April 12.[7] There is no official record of a concession from Tamaulipas, but Jean Louis Berlandier—a French naturalist attached to the Mexican boundary commission of 1828 who became a resident of Matamoros—mentions one,[8] and one was transferred in 1829. No record could be found of Nuevo Leon's action. It seemed that the Rio Grande, at last, was to respond to the dreams of Santa María and the recommendations of Calleja.

How far upriver their steamboat expedition got is unrecorded. Some-one reported to Berlandier that they failed to reach Camargo, but that is unlikely when one considers the depth of channel below Mier, even in low water. It may have taken them to the falls of the Rio Grande; it is more probable, however, that they either reached the broad sand and gravel shoal above the Rio Salado or a ledge below Laredo. William H. Egerton, writing in 1835, reported that one boat that had reached the ledge was pre-ceded by another that went beyond Camargo.[9]

It was probably this exploration that caused Bradburn and Staples to insist on a mix of horse-drawn boats and steamers. Opening the river from Chihuahua to the Devil's River would enable horse-drawn boats to ferry goods to that point, where small steamers could be used to the falls and put aboard larger steamers—along with goods from Coahuila. In low water, horse-drawn boats could substitute for the steamers and continue down to the ledge before transferring goods to steamers for the final leg to Matamoros.

Evidence indicates that Bradburn stayed on the lower river while Staples proceeded upriver to Chihuahua. Perhaps they intended to start opening the river from both ends, planning to meet somewhere between. But fate intervened. In 1829 the Spanish attempted to reconquer Mexico. Bradburn was called to duty. The Spanish were defeated by Santa Anna.[10]

Work was suspended. The state of Chihuahua lamented: "Even less is hope here today since the suspension of making the Rio Grande [navi-gable] . . . and the realization of which would be perhaps the only way to revive our commerce; it would take our commerce forward in a thousand ways. The door to opening the Rio Grande must not be closed."[11]

Suspension of the project took place a full year before state conces-sions were to expire if steam or horse-drawn boats were not in service. Because of political unrest and chaos, the partners sought and received a national six-month extension but were unsuccessful in getting another. The Tamaulipas grant was transferred to Henry Austin; the Coahuila and Texas concession—which Austin also wanted—expired; Chihuahua, ever hopeful, kept the grant intact.

Henry Austin seems to have been a cantankerous, impatient fortune hunter. A cousin of Stephen F. Austin, one of the first *norteamericano* colonizers of Texas, he had lost one fortune and was doing his best to recoup and create another. He acquired the *Ariel,* a small, deep-drafted steamboat apparently built on the order of those designed by his friend and onetime roommate, Robert Fulton, for western rivers. Austin came to the Rio Grande in August 1829,[12] not one of the more sublime seasons in the subtropics. His crew came down with cholera, making it virtually impossible to traffic upriver, and he discovered that his steamboat had too much draft to ascend the river above Mier. He told Berlandier that she drew three and a half feet, but his pilot, Alpheus Rackliffe, stated that she needed more than five feet of water to navigate.[13] There being no usable landing at Mier, Austin was restricted to trade between Camargo, Reynosa, and Matamoros. The ill health of his crew, his vessel's deep draft, and his own impatience led to a loss the first season. In the spring of 1830, he managed to break even, but his innate distrust of the Mexican character, his gruffness, and his impatience caused him to decide to leave the Rio Grande and try fortune-hunting along the Brazos River, in his cousin's colony. He wrote Stephen F. Austin that he was coming, requested influence in securing a large grant, and departed.

Alpheus Rackliffe stayed on the Rio Grande. He was young—twenty at the time—and possessed an adventurous spirit combined with the Yankee shrewdness that seems to accompany Maine men wherever they go.[14] Almost immediately, he got a commission to survey the Rio Grande. The survey was to consist of charting channel width, river width, channel depth, and bank heights at least to the Sierra Blanca—a mountain chain in Chihuahua across the Rio Grande from the town of Sierra Blanca and the mountain peak of the same name. He got that far, and there are indications that he may have gone beyond El Paso. His journal is not clear as to which state ordered the survey, but it may have been Chihuahua. All Rackliffe wrote was that a "government official" paid for the survey.

Rackliffe then put his knowledge of the river to good use. He ordered some keelboats (variously referred to as *flatboats* and *barges*), probably from New Orleans, and went into the freighting business on the Rio Grande, usually running from Presidio del Rio Grande to Matamoros and points between. It was on one of these trips that he first saw the young woman who was to entrap him and keep him on the river. He had fallen in love with María Trinidad, the daughter of Andrés Treviño-Gutiérrez of Laredo and Guerrero. (Rackliffe frequently described her in his journals as "the most beautiful girl" he had ever seen.) Two years after he first saw her, they were married. His freighting business prospered until the political strife of the interior spilled to the banks of the Rio Grande. He then took up the practice of medicine—at first in Guerrero, and then, after the Mexican War, in Brownsville. Apparently finding medicine an unprofitable profession, he bought some business property in Laredo in 1855, moved his family there, and set up business as a merchant-rancher. He also continued to use the river for trade.

His choice of keelboats over steamers was based on his intimate knowledge of the river. The Rio Grande had a much faster current than the Mississippi;[15] it required a keel, not a spoon-bottom powered by low-pressure steam, to buck it properly, especially in bends. His boats, once described as being capable of carrying 125 men each, were not as large as steamers and had a smaller cargo capacity. But they were much cheaper to operate and did not demand the huge cargoes that steamers did to show a profit—an important point. Profits could be made with a keelboat. The meager produce of the Rio Grande towns and countryside would have made steamers a losing proposition. He was not interested in the Mexican trade, as others would be; he was interested in a *river* trade. Rackliffe had faith in the Great River's economic future.

So did William Egerton, a surveyor for the Rio Grande and Texas Land Company, who saw two of Rackliffe's boats in 1834 and picked up on their importance. Attempting to show that the river was passable at Las Islitas (falls of the Rio Grande), he wrote:

I, however, knew that two moderate *sized* flat boats had actually passed at low water from above the ledge I have spoken of amongst "las islitas" and so on to Matamoros, and having obtained a guide who had been acquainted with all the localities of the place for upwards of twenty years, I spent the whole day in the water [at Las Islitas] in a laborious but interesting examination and had the satisfaction to see the seemingly great and numerous obstacles gradually diminish until they resolved themselves into one, comparatively but trifling, the only difficulty being to pass the great ledge.[16]

Rackliffe's economic success, the foresight of men like Egerton, and the prospects of profit from Mexican trade brought more steamboats to the Great River. In 1833 the *Tangipahoa* appeared in Matamoros, in spite of the ban on ships. It may have been the ban that caused her to be placed in Mexican owners' registry.[17] Eighteen thirty-four was a good year for steamers. Another appeared at Matamoros, and—auguring well for the future— a steamer landed at Laredo.[18] In 1837, probably as a result of the lifting of the ban against boats at Matamoros, yet another riverboat made that town its home port. Despite the successes of the early steamers, though, and despite the successes of Rackliffe and the enthusiasm of Egerton, the Rio Grande, which seemed to be on the verge of becoming a second Mississippi, was to be denied her destiny once more. Eighteen thirty-five was the last year of peace the river would know until the American military marched down from the north to subdue and annex the north and east banks.

By 1832 the economic situation under Bustamante had become so desperate that Santa Anna turned to the Federalists and helped them overthrow the Centralist dictator. Elections were held under the Federalist constitution of 1824; Santa Anna was elected president, and a long-time fighter for federalism and reform, Valentín Gómez Farías, was elected vice-president. In 1833 Santa Anna, claiming to be ill, retired to his estate, and Farías became president.

The Farías government immediately put into effect reforms that could have at least temporarily solved some of the economic problems facing the nation. The Catholic church was stripped of its privileged status; the army was reduced in size and power; and a revamped colonial policy was established. Restrictive laws concerning the origin of settlers (particularly in Texas) instituted by Bustamante were remanded; states were allowed to establish their own colonization laws within a broad framework; Texas was to be separated from Coahuila and given statehood. (The *tejanos* even went so far as to elect a governor-to-be, write a constitution, and establish a state judicial system.) By allowing the states more freedom in determining their own destinies, the Federalist government immediately cut its expenses; allowing the Anglo-Saxon Tejanos to establish a state in which all were equally at liberty was the one way to save that northern province. The Federalist experiment brought Mexico her first real revolution. It lasted less than a year.

Perhaps one example of the tribulations created by the intrigues and changes of government and policy is best illustrated by the fate of the colony of Dolores, established near the Rio Grande in 1834 by Dr. John Charles Beales, English born and a graduate of the Royal College of Surgeons.[19] Upon graduation, he came to Mexico to set up his practice in the capital city, married the widow of a friend, and thus acquired a huge colonization grant that included most of what is today west Texas.

A stock company was formed—the Rio Grande and Texas Land Company—and Charles Edwards, a New York attorney, was named agent. Dr. Beales went to Europe to seek colonists while Edwards sought settlers from the northeastern United States. In 1832, while Beales and Edwards were seeking profit through colonization, the state of Coahuila and Texas passed a liberal colonization law that encouraged settlement and economic development. Edwards had it translated, added some information of his own, and published it in 1834, stressing the navigability of the Rio Grande. In an undated publication that described the location of the proposed new settlement, Edwards expanded on the theme of navigation: "The Rio Grande . . . by which the grants now settling are bounded, is navigable for steamboats, up and down, for seven months, at least, of the year, mainly from May to December; and flat boats can go down it nearly at all times."[20]

In Europe, Beales secured colonists from Ireland, England, and Germany. The group sailed to Aransaco (Aransas) Bay, trekked overland to San Antonio, then southwest to a point on Las Moras Creek, twelve miles up from its confluence with the Rio Grande and seventy miles upriver from Presidio del Rio Grande. Egerton had selected the site for the settlement, but the initial colony failed. Thomas Power, a friend of Beales's and one of the colonists, felt that the failure was due to the arid climate and the inability of the Las Moras to provide enough water for irrigation. Eduard Ludecas seems to have blamed the failure more on the "impolitic behavior" of Egerton, left in charge of the colony by Beales.[21] Both may be correct. As long as Beales was with the settlers, all seemed to go well; but when he was forced to leave, quarrels broke out. Egerton could not, or did not know how to, exert leadership, and the result was failure. The first colony of Dolores broke up in the summer of 1834.

The importance of the Dolores colony to the Rio Grande lies not in its failure, but in the causes of that failure. The initial colony failed not because of the arid climate, or even a quarrelsome atmosphere, but because the Mexican economy could not support such an organized, well-thought-out venture. Such endeavors required capital that Mexico could not supply. Even though he had letters of credit from American and Mexican banks, Beales could not realize any support for them. Money was not available in either San Antonio or Monclova. He had to leave his colony and journey to a foreign land to secure the cash necessary to ensure survival. The initial crop loss could have been alleviated, too, if the state of Coahuila had been able to assist the settlers. It could not; it had no resources with which to help them. The benefits of the Federalist reforms had not yet reached the states. Egerton at least recognized *that* part of the problem and penned an eloquent report to the company's shareholders in New York. It was a document that emphasized the role the Rio Grande had to play if settlement was to succeed on its banks.

"The most important object is, after all, the *down* navigation as a means of conveying the surplus produce to a market, and this is not problematic, *for it has already been done. . . .* No place can offer a finer market than Matamoros, to which the produce would float down in flat boats, which on their arrival there could be sold for more than their cost."[22]

Berlandier, writing about the same time, penned a proposal for the use of three types of boats on the river: large steamers to go to Mier, smaller ones on to Laredo, and still smaller ones to Presidio del Rio Grande.[23] Berlandier felt that once the boats were on the river, settlement and economic development would be assured. With certain knowledge of flatboat traffic and a fledgling steamboat trade on the lower river, more and more citizens of the Rio Grande began looking to the river as a source of rescue from their economic doldrums. Far upriver from Dolores colony, the state of Chihuahua decided that the Rio Grande was so important to it that J. A. Escudero, an official of the state, wrote in *Noticias estadísticas (Statistical Information)*, "We must consider the Rio Grande or Rio del Norte as one of the most important natural resources of the Republic, and especially of the interior states."

There followed an accurate description of the navigable river to near the Conchos. "From the mountain [unidentified in the report, but probably Eagle's Tail Mountain, 147 miles downstream from El Paso]," he added, "to El Paso del Norte the river has been plumbed to fix with certitude the river capacity for navigation; the reports . . . give a very favorable idea of its navigability for a great part of the year to El Paso del Norte . . . with boats of a size sufficient to transport [merchandise and agricultural products] of the state." It may have been Rackliffe's survey that fixed the limits of navigation. Escudero concludes, "From this point to New Mexico we cannot speak with the same certainty with respect to the small size or large size of boats, but it can be said that it is navigable for small boats in time of high water."[24] The report completes the navigable exploration of the Rio Grande to 1834. It had been established that the river was navigable by steamboat from the Gulf of Mexico to the Devil's River; there follows a 350-mile stretch of rapids, falls, and obstacles running through Santa Elena Canyon to Eagle's Tail Mountain, but from that point to Santo Domingo some form of navigation was possible. Those who followed Fr. Vicente Santa María and Teodoro Ortiz y Ayala had laid a foundation for making their prophesies come true.

Such effort and evidence was wasted. President Farías was overthrown. The church, education, and military reforms instituted by his government had alienated Federalist allies among those powerful classes; they united to establish Santa Anna as the president and dictator of Mexico and to restore privilege.

The Mexican states were infuriated by the destruction of the constitution of 1824. Some, like Zacatecas, rose in open revolt. The Supreme Congress of Coahuila and Texas called upon all Mexican states to join in resisting Santa Anna and forbade him and his troops to enter the state. The Texans waited. After all, they had sided with Santa Anna in overthrowing Bustamante. Many felt that Santa Anna would support the reforms that would alleviate their condition.

The states were helpless. Those that resisted the military power of Santa Anna were crushed. Santa Anna sent his brother-in-law, General

Martín Perfecto de Cos, to San Antonio with an army. The Texans were to be reminded that authoritarianism was the new order. Cos so alienated the Texans that they rose up in a Federalist rebellion that was actually created by Santa Anna's lust for power. On Christmas Eve, 1835, Cos and his army crossed the Rio Grande at Laredo. In exchange for parole, he and his soldiers had given their word that they would never oppose Texas again. The Texans continued to operate as if the constitution of 1824 were still in force. They were joined by Mexican patriots and Federalists who were despondent and desperate, men such as Lorenzo de Zavala, who had been the minister of the treasury, the governor of the state of Mexico twice, and an ardent Federalist. He was to become the first vice-president of the Republic of Texas, for Santa Anna's actions turned an attempt to restore constitutional rule into a rebellion that eventually cost Mexico her northern provinces from Texas to California. Ortiz y Ayala proved to be correct. Mexico had much to fear from the United States. She had more to fear from Santa Anna's ruthless ambition.

Before Santa Anna crossed the Great River at Presidio del Rio Grande, he sent word to a new group of settlers at Dolores: "Get out, foreigners," it said in effect, "or suffer." Santa Anna's power-hungry dictum did more than destroy a fledgling colony of "foreigners." It also denied the upper Rio Grande a chance at steamboat navigation, for the Rio Grande and Texas Land Company had the resources—and the intent—to open the river.[25]

Santa Anna lost the Texas War, as it came to be called in Mexico. Texas Became a separate and sovereign nation, recognized not only by the United States but also by European powers. The first act of her new Congress was to declare the Rio Grande, from its mouth to its headwaters and beyond, as her boundary with Mexico. Texas was as powerless to enforce such a claim as Mexico was to retake Texas. The result was a six-year period of border warfare centering on the Rio Grande, and renewed Centralist-Federalist struggles revolving around Laredo.

The Rio Grande also became the scene of Mexican attack and Texan counterattack during most of the period. Deaf Smith, the famed Texas Army scout, led two expeditions to capture Laredo and place it in the hands of Texas; the citizens of Laredo and Guerrero, along with many others who constituted the Rio Grande community, raised the flag of federalism in 1839. When their attempt to return to the constitution of 1824 was put down in a bloody series of minibattles, they raised the flag of independence. The Republic of the Rio Grande was born at the Orevena Ranch (near modern Zapata) on January 18, 1840. After some initial battlefield successes, it was crushed in November of the same year.

It is no wonder that the striving river towns and provinces, just beginning to achieve a semblance of economic success, suddenly withered. What little trade there was on the river became a smuggling trade between Texan and Mexican merchants; on the lower river, Matamoros prospered as a contraband port, delivering little to the Centralist coffers and supplying much of interior Mexico with its wares. River trade, just beginning to recover from the Texas War, was tragically brought to a halt.

Mexico's leaders were unable to admit that Texas was indeed a free and sovereign nation; they dreamed of reestablishing themselves in that vast land. Small raiding parties rode north from Matamoros, undetected in the unpopulated brush country, to strike at Texas frontier settlements and frontier trade. Despite the outcries of editorialists and citizens, the leaders of Texas wisely refrained, for the most part, from mounting retaliatory actions. The Texas economy needed peace, not war. By 1838 Mexican raiding parties on the frontier were becoming more than bothersome. The *Matagorda Bulletin* ran a story about one such raid, and in the best tradition of what Mark Twain called "Arkansaw journalism," editorialized about it.

The reporter, after describing the killing of citizens and the theft of freight wagons and goods, was intent on arousing action. He pointed out that this was the second raid in recent months and that the raids would not cease until Matamoros was taken and military posts were established on the Texas bank of the Rio Grande. Apparently he felt that more evidence was needed to convince many of his readers, for he added, most forcibly, "Texas should have the exclusive navigation of that river, and this we cannot obtain except by conquest."[26]

Texas could not sustain the effort needed for conquest. Neither could Mexico. The story stressed navigation on the Rio Grande. It was a thing to be desired, a reason for conquest.

For the next few years, Texas knew a small respite. Warfare on the Rio

The Mier expedition floats down the Rio Grande. The lithographer ignored Green's description of the boats, each capable of carrying 125 men. From Thomas Jefferson Green, *Journal of the Texian Expedition against Mier* (1844).

Grande, so readily joined by Texas volunteers, interfered with raids. Then, in 1842, General Adrian Woll of the Mexican army led a raid on San Antonio. He got away without a fight and with the town's city council as prisoners. The citizens of Texas were enraged, embarrassed, and frustrated. President Sam Houston ordered an army under General Alexander Sommervell to the field to punish Texas's neighbor republic. Laredo was taken and looted, and then the loot was returned. Sommervell ordered his troops home. Many refused, wanting to take Matamoros. The result was the Mier Expedition, which went down in history as a military defeat for the Texans but a moral victory after Santa Anna ordered every tenth man shot.

One of the survivors of the expedition was Thomas Jefferson Green, a Texas congressman and a fervent believer in union with the United States. It was on the Mier expedition that Green first saw the Rio Grande. After taking Laredo, the army marched down the east bank of the river to a point opposite the Rio Salado, near which lay the town of Guerrero. Here, at a

Carrizo Indian village where the two rivers met, six large flatboats were taken, along with several smaller boats. Green was appointed commander of the newly acquired "navy." Each boat was capable of carrying 125 men, which meant a surplus of boats; those not needed for transport were burned. And so the renegade army floated down the Rio Grande to the entrance of the Rio Alamo. The river was impressive.

> We descended it at a low stage of water—in few occasions does it get lower—and never found any place at which it could be forded below Laredo, and it is, indeed, barely fordable there. [It was December 1842.] It is a beautiful river, averaging four hundred yards in width, with high bluffs generally on one side or the other, and the opposite side always a fertile bottom. This river resembles more the Ohio, when in boatable order, than any we recollect to have seen and is far superior for steamboat navigation to any other upon the Gulf of Mexico west of the Mississippi.[27]

Green adds, "The flotilla proceeded down the river, capturing and burning forty or fifty boats." Before the troops advanced on Mier—and faced ultimate defeat—the flatboats were destroyed. Alpheus Rackliffe's dreams were destroyed, too.

Alarmed at the events in both Texas and Mexico, the British were moved to take some kind of action. It was not in the best interests of the British, as they saw them, to allow such warfare to continue. Texas, England felt, must be preserved as an independent nation; Mexico must be aided in coming to a similar decision. Amid deteriorating Anglo-Mexican relations, the English consul-general to the Republic of Texas, Charles Elliott (later to become Admiral Sir Charles Elliott) penned a lengthy letter to Lord Aberdeen, head of the Foreign Office: "The river [Rio Grande] . . . is illfitted for . . . military transport, being shallow in the dry season, and . . . having rapids, before that point [Presidio del Rio Grande]. . . . In the winter and Spring Months, the Rio Grande would be navigable for a great distance in light boats, such as are used in the upper Ganges and Indus."[28]

Elliott had the high-water months wrong, and his information about navigability in low water was also incorrect, at least below Mier. It is strange that he had not received better information. William Kennedy, who was to become British consul at Galveston, had quoted Egerton's reports verbatim in *The Rise, Prospects, and Progress of the Republic of Texas*, then in its second edition. Elliott's misinformation was not critical, though. The British were preparing for a possible war that centralism's antiforeign policies—created partly by Britain's Texas policy—seemed to be generating.

The Rio Grande, it appeared, was going to know a substantial river traffic—if not commercial, then naval. And a military flotilla did appear, in 1846; but it was American, not British. Texas joined the United States, and war came to the Rio Grande—as did the United States Army Quartermaster Department, the U.S.Q.M.D.

U.S.Q.M.D.

The annexation of Texas by the United States led to a brief, bloody war between the two powers of North America. The war was a mismatch from its beginning. Mexico was in poor economic condition and could not sustain the effort necessary to fight the United States successfully. Her political wars had created intense distrust among the military, and her dilapidated systems of communication and transportation preordained the conclusion. Mexico did not have the slightest chance of winning the war, despite superior numbers.

The beginning of the war showed that. General Zachary Taylor marched his small army to the north bank of the Rio Grande, left a detachment at an improvised "Fort Texas" (opposite Matamoros), and took the remainder of his army back toward Point Isabel, fearing a movement to separate his army from its logistical base. Badly outnumbered, he defeated the Mexicans at Palo Alto on May 8, 1846, and the next day routed them at Resaca de la Palma. A lack of boats and pontoon bridges prevented the immediate taking of Matamoros and the total destruction of the Mexican army that had faced him. When he had gotten across the Rio Grande, though, he had but one idea in mind: crush the enemy. In order to do that, he needed transportation—steamboats to get his troops and supplies upriver to Camargo, the jumping-off point for Monterrey, and mule trains to carry supplies while the army marched. The American economy supplied both. So efficient was the Quartermaster Department, in fact, that a shipyard was built near the mouth of the river that could not only repair ships, but also build boats.[1]

The war's importance to the Rio Grande cannot be overestimated. The *norteamericanos* who came to the river in 1846 were part of a water transport and communication tradition; many had depended on southern or western rivers or the Mississippi before becoming embroiled in troop movements and supply problems on the Brave River. The pilots and captains who answered the call for experienced riverboatmen were a hardy, risk-taking group who felt that a boat could go anywhere "a dry creek flows."[2] One of these was Captain Mark Sterling of Pittsburgh, who came to the Rio Grande in 1846 to command a quartermaster riverboat, the *Major Brown*. When the army determined that the Rio Grande would have to be explored thoroughly, at least as far as Presidio del Rio Grande, the *Major Brown* got the nod. She was a 125-ton sidewheeler, 150 feet long, with a beam of forty-six feet over the guards, and a draft, loaded, of three feet.[3] She seemed ideal for such a journey. Lieutenant Bryant P. Tilden of the 3rd Infantry was placed in command of the troops stationed aboard her.[4]

The expedition began in October 1846. Unaware of the pulsating periods of high and low water, Sterling and Tilden had to rely on advice that the river was in low water. Ordinarily it would have been, but the late summer and early fall of 1846 were extraordinarily wet in the Mexican mountains that fed the Great River's tributaries, and the river was in middle stage. All the way upriver it kept dropping. From Camargo to Guerrero (formerly Revilla), there were no serious obstacles. The only problem was the inability of mesquite logs to produce heat enough for a high head of steam. Coal, Tilden felt, was a prerequisite to Rio Grande navigation.

At Guerrero, Alpheus Rackliffe joined the expedition. He turned his charts and maps over to Tilden, expecting them to be made available to the American public. Just after entering the Rio Grande from the Rio Salado, the *Major Brown* met her first obstacle, a sand and gravel shoal that barred passage around an island. As Tilden described it, "The boat grounded at the foot of a large island, having apparently plenty of water on each side . . . but it was ascertained that points of rock were standing straight up from the bottom."[5]

The river dropped three feet overnight. The next morning, a party was sent out to check the river further up, lest such conditions continue. When the party returned, it reported that there was clear water ahead. It took two days to pull the *Major Brown* over the sand and gravel bar. The river was then clear, except for a ledge that spanned the river about twenty miles above the Salado. It stretched, said Tilden, "diagonally across the river for one mile in extent. Over this reef, the water falls in some places two feet.

And just below its centre, nearest the American shore, is a passage of a hundred feet or more, through which the main body of the water passes." This was the "great ledge" below Laredo that Egerton had written of. Further up, the boat passed a series of reefs jutting out from the Mexican shore, but with good water on the American side. While making this passage, lack of power caused the boat to hang between the double reef fifteen miles below Laredo. Only the skill of Captain Sterling prevented a serious accident. Power, Tilden noted again, was required for the Rio Grande.

From the double reef, the river was clear of serious obstacles, but low water held the *Major Brown* at Laredo for several weeks. Luckily, winter rains—an unusual phenomenon—brought a rise in the river, and she was back at work for the army in March. Had the river followed its usual period of high water, the *Major Brown* would have been there until May. She had too much beam for a channel averaging twenty-two feet in width and too much draft for a falling or low stage of the river.

Rather than risk the boat in low water, Tilden, Rackliffe, and others rode horses to Presidio del Rio Grande; Tilden meant to examine the river between there and Laredo. At Presidio del Rio Grande, Rackliffe left the party, taking charge of the horses and returning to Laredo. Tilden's group could have used his knowledge of the channel in Las Islitas. Perhaps Rackliffe did not relish the thought of going through them in low water, although he had made passage many times during the summer rise. In high water Egerton had found them passable except for one ledge. Tilden, who explored them in low water, was amazed at the number of islands, reefs, and ledges that barred passage. He could discover no channel. Tilden was even more amazed when told that Mexicans in flatboats made the trip regularly.

Because the army, for some reason, received no notes or charts or reports from Tilden, it sent a topographical engineer up the river on a survey a year later.[6] He recommended that the river be opened, at least to keelboats, to within 150 land miles of El Paso. His report did not say so directly, but he suspected that once he was able to get around a great ledge at that point, the river might be opened even further. (The state of Chihuahua had already determined that, but the army did not know it.)

The war also brought Mifflin Kenedy, Richard King, and Brevet Major

W. W. Chapman to the Rio Grande. Along with Charles Stillman, a Matamoros merchant and agent, they would dictate the future of the Rio
Grande.[7] Stillman had arrived in Matamoros in 1828, an eighteen-year-old
youth. A year earlier, his father—a Connecticut merchant—had sent him
to Durango to serve as the company factor; he was sent to Matamoros to
serve in the same capacity. He made an amazing profit and found his life's
work: making money. He did so devoutly, becoming wealthy and, at the
same time, increasing the family coffers back in Connecticut.

Chapman came to the river in 1847, and in April 1848 he became assistant quartermaster in charge of the army's steamers.[8] It was his job to
use them efficiently to get troops downriver and homeward bound. He had
been breveted to major as a result of "gallant and meritorious conduct" at
the Battle of Buena Vista, then was made aide-de-camp to Brevet Major
General Wool before being assigned to the Rio Grande.

Captain Mifflin Kenedy arrived in the summer of 1846. A Florida river
skipper, he had taken his steamboat up to Pittsburgh for repairs that spring
from its home base on the Chattahoochee River, leaving behind his pilot, a
young but mature Richard King. While he was in Pittsburgh, he got involved in helping the army select riverboats for General Taylor's army, then
encamped at Matamoros. One thing led to another, and Kenedy found
himself on the Great River, commanding the *Corvette,* built as a luxury
passenger liner but bought by the army for VIP use during the war.

The last to arrive was Richard King. Kenedy wrote him from the river,
telling him of the money to be earned and inviting him to join the civilian
corps of captains and pilots on army boats. After he arrived, King served as
a pilot before getting his own command, the *Colonel Cross.*

In order to comprehend Chapman and his initial enthusiasm for opening the river, one must closely examine the army's problems following the
Mexican War. The Treaty of Guadalupe-Hidalgo, which ended the war,
pledged the United States to protect Mexico from pillaging Indian war parties that habitually crossed the Rio Grande from Texas. In order to comply
with the treaty, the government established a series of military posts along
the river: Fort Brown (which preceded the treaty, having been erected as
"Fort Texas"), and Ringgold Barracks (at Clay Davis's Landing), Fort McIntosh (west of Laredo), and Fort Duncan (near the site of a new town named

Eagle Pass). Quartermaster General Thomas S. Jessup decided to supply them from the depot at Brazos Santiago, which had been built during the war. It would be Chapman's job to see that the new posts were properly supplied.

He also had to dispose of surplus army property—and that included riverboats that had managed to survive the tortuous Rio Grande. As he undertook his dual job, he looked around for some help. The shipping firm of Bodman and Clark expressed an interest in carrying government troops and supplies up to Ringgold Barracks. Chapman wrote Jessup on December 28, 1848, in response to a query about private transportation: "[I] have conversed with several persons interested in steamboats on the Rio Grande,—and learned today that it is in contemplation by some of the principal merchants of Brownsville—and owners of steamboats, including Bodman and Clark, to form a company for the purpose of establishing a line of steamboats between the Brazos and Roma, some thirty miles above Camargo. In case this line is formed, . . . it will probably purchase the boat houses, and foundry at the mouth of the river."[9]

Bodman and Clark were merchants, commission agents, and boat owners who had their offices in the "floating hotel *Frankland*" at the mouth of the river. The firm operated the steamer *Laurel* on a twice-weekly basis between Matamoros and the mouth of the river, Captain Lund commanding. The *Laurel* had an excellent reputation for the table it set.[10] The firm's primary interest lay in lightering off Brazos Island and in towing incoming schooners over the bar for off-loading. Bodman and Clark knew the boat business.

Another privately owned steamboat on the river was the *Tom Kirkman,* under the command of Captain Dowd. She was owned by Stillman, and she plied between Matamoros and Camargo. Stillman was a businessman in the classic nineteenth-century mold. He saw business as having no social responsibilities, only profitable ones. As a result, he had his hand in many pies with as many different associates. He and his New York partners, among them James Jewett, had formed the New York and Brownsville Improvement Company, Ltd., to found the town of Brownsville; locally he had put together the Brownsville Town Company to market it. He operated warehouses, mercantile businesses, and a forwarding company. He put in a ferry service between Matamoros and his new town, eventually using a fine brick warehouse (built by and at one time owned by Major Chapman) at the Texas end of it.

He recognized quickly that a port facility opposite Matamoros would siphon off the business that had made that Mexican city so attractive to American and European businessmen. After all, the United States now controlled the only anchorage that could serve either the new town or Matamoros—Brazos Santiago and Point Isabel. Stillman's acute business sense led him to enter the steamboat service, operating boats up and down the river even before the Mexican War came to an end. He was as interested as Bodman and Clark were in any government contract that might materialize, and he did not feel that any competition for that contract should trouble him. Highly intelligent, quick-witted, and affable, he may have sensed one method of securing a contract; it may be coincidence that Chapman took certain actions that led to a noncompetitive contract. The former is more likely.

Stillman did not like competition. It cost money. To him the only business venture worth trying was one in which the competition could be neutralized, by either buying it out or driving it out.

Following the letter of December 28, Chapman's correspondence was concerned mainly with the disposing of government property, including surplus steamboats. He was also deeply concerned about the responsibility of supplying the river posts and was constantly aware of the cost involved. He familiarized himself, as much as possible, with prior attempts to navigate or survey the river. After all, it was an economic fact of transport and communication that waterways meant comparative speed and considerably less cost than any other method.

In all the correspondence between Chapman and General Jessup, the only mention of private contractors taking over the supply job is in one letter. It would be eighteen months or so before the idea came up again. Major Chapman was preoccupied with disposing of property and supplying the river posts. As early as October 1848, headquarters in San Antonio was querying Chapman about both. On the thirty-first he wrote a businesslike letter to Major Tompkins, the departmental quartermaster, declaring that he had decided "to retain the *Major Brown* and the *Corvette* to run

Wrecked and disintegrated hull of a steamer—probably the *Corvette*, deliberately sunk at this site in February 1852. Courtesy Burt Johnson.

between the mouth of the Rio Grande and the upper posts." The *Mentoria* was being kept to run between the mouth of the river and Point Isabel and the *Yazoo* to run between Brazos Santiago and Point Isabel.

Chapman's letters to General Jessup, however, are less businesslike and more revealing. In November he told Jessup that "a town has grown up along side of [Fort Brown] since May, which now numbers two thousand inhabitants. Matamoros will go down and Brownsville will prosper, so long as the Mexican government keeps up its prohibitions and high tariffs. Smuggling is carried on most extensively all along the river."

While Chapman was wrestling with the problems of setting up a line of supply, principally by water, and the disposal of property, Mifflin Kenedy and Richard King were marking time. Kenedy went up to Roma to try his hand at real estate development, and King ran a bar and rooming house at the mouth of the river, near the quartermaster yard. Both had been snagged by the Rio Grande, and each felt that his future was on the river. Kenedy found, however, that real estate development at Roma was not as lucrative as Stillman's similar efforts downriver at Brownsville; King seemed to be waiting for the public auction of remaining boats.

After some delay, the auction was held on April 2 and 3, 1849. Bodman and Clark bought two boats, the *Brownsville* and the *J. E. Roberts*. The *Brownsville* was steaming up to Pittsburgh for a major overhaul when she snagged and sank, appropriately enough, in the Brownsville Chute of the Mississippi. The *J. E. Roberts*, being in good condition, remained on the Rio Grande. Bodman and Clark had also acquired the *Del Norte*, a large, deep-draft sternwheeler, and placed her in service. Samuel A. Belden bought the *Troy* and the *Whiteville*, among other vessels, ostensibly for himself but in reality to add to Stillman's fleet, operated under Belden's name after 1848. Mifflin Kenedy was put in charge of the *Troy*, and she began regular trips between Camargo, Roma, and Brownsville.[11] With some financial help from Robert Penny,[12] Richard King bought his old command, the *Colonel Cross*, and went into business for himself. His early knockabout years on southern rivers came in handy: he was able to be his own assistant engineer, accountant, captain, and pilot.

With the disposal of government steamboats out of the way, Chapman turned his attention to exploring the feasibility of supplying the river posts

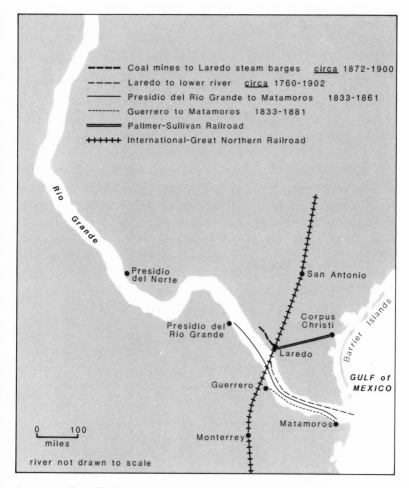

Attempts at River Trade

by water. On May 16 he sent a report to General Jessup concerning an exploration by Captain Daniel M. Kingsbury. The report has been lost, but a newspaper story in the *American Flag* of that date tells all about it.

"There are obstructions in the river [below Kingsbury's Falls]," the story says, "which would prevent its navigation about seven months of each year by steamboats of the class which now run between its mouth and Ringgold Barracks." The reporter is quick to point out, however, that the obstructions posed no problem for smaller steamers or keelboats and adds that in high water, reefs and shoals were no problem for any vessel. The story continues:

Kingsbury proceeded with the barge to within two leagues of Presidio, a distance of 130 miles above Laredo. At this place a cluster of rocks extending across the river presented an obstacle to present navigation above that point. . . .

Captain Kingsbury visited our camp at Eagle Pass, about 40 miles above Presidio. He reports the river as appearing well above this point, and the best information he could gather was that the river for several hundred miles above the Presidio was uninterrupted by any serious obstacles to navigation—decidedly better navigation than below—and the chain of rocks represented below Presidio was represented by the old citizens as the greatest impediment to the navigation of the river for a great distance.

Offers have been made to transport Government freight to our upper posts at prices much less than it could have been transported previously.

Chapman was more than pleased with the experiment. Aware of the 1847 survey of the river, he felt that Captain Kingsbury's report confirmed at least a portion of it. Chapman ordered good oak from New Orleans and began to plan a major exploration of the river. Meanwhile, he prepared to go to Washington to put his "public accounts in order." While he was there, he wrote Jessup about a follow-up to Kingsbury's exploration by a Captain Easterly, who returned confident that the Rio Grande was navigable to within 150 miles of El Paso once Kingsbury's Falls was cleared.

Chapman then informed Jessup that two additional keelboats were being built to run between Laredo and that point on the river. "We may be able," he added, "after carrying our supplies around them [the obstacles] in wagons, to transport them further up the river in 'Anglia' class boats."

The savings in supplying and manning western posts would be tremendous, since all supplies for those posts were hauled overland from Lavaca, a distance of more than seven hundred miles. Chapman and the army were opening up the Rio Grande. His idea of using *Anglia*-class boats to

Las Islitas, falls of the Rio Grande. The cross marks the place where P. D. Cunningham, a consulting engineer with the International Boundary (Water) Commission survey, drowned. From *Equitable Distribution.* Courtesy Russell Brown.

get materials further upriver was sound. Officials of the state of Chihuahua had had the same idea fifteen years earlier.

While the assistant quartermaster was in Washington, Stillman was having his own problems. After buying up several surplus boats, he had hired James O'Donnell, a river captain for the army, as rivermaster. O'Donnell had his hands full. The old boats were in need of overhaul, and their boilers and machinery were in disrepair. There were no facilities on the river to do such work, except the army's, and to bring in needed parts was prohibitively expensive. O'Donnell found himself cannibalizing some boats in order to keep others running. Profits were nonexistent. Not a man to admit defeat or to throw good money after bad, Stillman sought a way out of his dilemma.

Of all the boats on the river, only those run by Bodman and Clark and by private captains—including Richard King and Robert Penny's *Colonel*

Cross—were showing profits. Competition was costing Charles Stillman money. It was apparent either that O'Donnell was not up to the task or that the task was beyond any amount of effort. Stillman had one virtue. If he felt no social responsibility, he was loyal to those who were loyal to him. O'Donnell kept running a money-losing enterprise.

Stillman got an idea. Kenedy was a river captain; he had a competitive spirit that O'Donnell lacked. Although Kenedy had turned command of the *Troy* over to Captain James B. Armstrong and abandoned the river for highly profitable trading ventures in Mexico, he might be the answer to the dilemma. Stillman called him in for a little talk. Kenedy listened, but he did not commit himself. Instead, he looked up Richard King, his friend and confidant. King, who had been thinking about the best way to conquer the river profitably, had some ideas himself.

Chapman was unaware of Stillman's problems and returned to the Brazos in January 1850, committed to opening up the Rio Grande to its ultimate limits. On the twenty-fourth he wrote the Eighth Department headquarters, outlining his plans for the future. "[One of the two keelboats] will be completed in fifteen days,—and the other soon after. As soon as the smaller one is ready, I shall direct Harry Love to take her and to ascend the Rio Grande to the highest possible point. The larger keel boat will be put in service, for the present, between Laredo and Eagle Pass. *I hope the engineers have cut the channel to the Falls below Presidio Rio Grande.*"

Opening the falls, he added, would allow the army to do away with the wagon trains that supplied Eagle Pass. It would also lead to a great influx of settlers, who would flock to the fertile Rio Grande with the advent of water transportation. To prove the viability of the river, he intended to send the *Major Brown* to the falls—and through them, if possible, with the coming spring rise. He concluded the letter: "I am quite sanguine in the belief we will yet be able to put on the upper Rio Grande a class of iron steamboats which will supercede the keel boats and save much labor and expense."

There is no evidence that the *Major Brown* made a second historic ascent of the Rio Grande. Perhaps the fact that private captains were beginning to call on Guerrero regularly and were inching their way farther and farther upriver—until at least two of them reached beyond Laredo to the falls[13]—led Chapman to believe that the experiment was unnecessary.

While the lower Rio Grande seemed ready to become a second Mississippi, in its upper reaches above Santa Fe and in Colorado the river was beginning to attract a few settlers who saw the irrigation works of the former Mexican citizens who lived there. The new settlers had installed improved irrigation works of their own, leading the way to more efficient use of water and more productive crops. Each year more water was taken from the upper river during her flood and high-water season. Each year, less water reached the lower river than had reached it the year before. The results of the Mexican War not only brought the possibility of navigation, with some portage, into New Mexico, but it brought the farmers who saw the river as a giver of life, not as a highway. The two viewpoints would live together in harmony, for a while, then clash in a tumultuous farewell to commercial and military boating on the Rio Grande.

Nemesis

Chapter 4

While the irrigationists of the upper reaches were beginning to expand their use of the river, lower-river traders, merchants, and the United States Army were using the river as a highway for trade, prosperity, and supply. Brazos Santiago had become the principal port for supplying northern Mexico all the way to Chihuahua with foreign goods and was the funnel through which exportable Mexican products found their way to world markets. Cheap water transportation made Camargo and Mier transshipping ports, Matamoros and Brownsville the terminus of trade, and Brazos Santiago its anchorage.

Most private captains and owners restricted themselves to this route, many of them making Camargo their furthest port of call. Mier's landing facilities were poor, and the Alamo River entrance was extremely narrow. Although Guerrero was easily attainable, that city was off the land trade route from Nuevo Leon to Camargo and therefore offered little profitable trade. It was a Mexican trade, actually, not a river trade; the river's produce was meager and unprofitable, as some private captains learned when they pushed their boats beyond Mier and Guerrero to Laredo and even to Kingsbury's Falls. These captains returned to the lower river with a single-minded message: there was neither produce nor profit upriver that could not be obtained, at much less cost, downriver.

Others on the lower river might have found prosperity in steamboating, but Charles Stillman did not. Searching for a way to make profits, he had talked to Kenedy, whose sagacity he respected. Kenedy, in turn, had talked to Richard King, who had ideas about profitmaking on the river. It would take specially designed boats—one for the Brazos to the mouth of the river run, another for upriver use; the former a broad-beamed husky cargo carrier carting just enough fuel to get from Brazos to Boca del Rio, the latter with powerful steammaking boilers that could provide high-pressure steam to drive her in the narrow bends and fast currents of the Rio Grande. Oper-

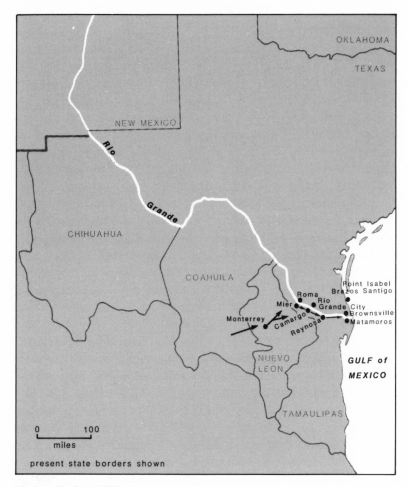

Mexican Trade to 1881

ated in tandem, the two could cut costs, run faster, and deliver more cargo than conventional boats. King sold the idea to Kenedy, who in turn sold it to Stillman. A new company was formed on March 1, 1850, comprising Stillman, O'Donnell, Kenedy, and King and Penny as equal partners.[1] King designed the boats; Kenedy went up to Pittsburgh to order their construction.

While Stillman was putting together his new moneymaking venture, he took time to introduce Brevet Major W. W. Chapman to the glories of real estate speculation. Chapman bought his first piece of property on February 20, 1850, a month after returning from Washington and just a few days before his optimistic report went out to both San Antonio and Jessup. It was at the corner of Eleventh and Elizabeth, adjoining Fort Brown. The sellers were Basse and Hord, attorneys who were assisting Stillman in his attempt to claim the Matamoros Commons, an important part of his Brownsville development. A. C. Allen immediately began constructing a fine brick warehouse on the lot, referring to it as "Chapman's warehouse."[2] Next, on April 3, he purchased half of the adjoining lot from Antonio Vancaral, a businessman. Stillman purchased the lots and the warehouse from Chapman on June 8. A few months later he sold them to Stephen Powers, who then sold them back to Chapman. Chapman reacquired them as separate purchases on January 8 and October 27, 1851. At the time, Powers was the steamboat company's attorney as well as the private attorney of both Stillman and King. When Chapman rebought the lots and the warehouse, he gave mortgage deeds for them. He surrendered one lot, with the warehouse, to Powers in 1852. The other he kept.

The Allen brothers, Sam and A. C., got in on the action, too. On May 5, 1850, A. C. sold Sam and Chapman a business lot downtown; the same day Chapman bought Sam's half and owned it all. On July 10, he sold half the lot back to Sam.

The fastest turnaround came in 1852. On June 28 Chapman bought two lots in Point Isabel from William Leitch. He sold them back to Leitch the same day, taking a mortgage.[3] Chapman was transferred to San Antonio about the time of the Leitch transactions, and few speculations took place in Cameron County afterwards. In the minds of some, these land dealings raised serious questions about Chapman's integrity. Apparently, though, Chapman found real estate profitable.

At the time he began trading real estate, Chapman was trying to get the Rio Grande opened up. By the time of the Leitch transactions, he had deliberately abandoned his efforts. But in early 1850, he was deeply involved in getting the Rio Grande opened to the Devil's River.

Captain Harry Love finally got off on his exploration of the river on

March 11, 1850. His keelboat had no problems reaching Laredo, and it got over the falls with comparative ease. At Eagle Pass, or Fort Duncan, the *Major Babbitt* stayed a few days, and Harry Love met the Cazneaus, founders and developers of the town. William L. Cazneau had been commissary-general of Texas under President Mirabeau Lamar. He hailed from Boston and had come to Texas before the revolution to become a cotton farmer. In 1845 he had served as a member of the Texas Constitutional Convention; in addition, he and his wife were good friends of Thomas Jefferson Green, who undoubtedly influenced their decision to enter the town-development business on the Rio Grande.

Jane McManus Storms Cazneau came from a politically influential New York family. She was highly intelligent and strong-willed and had created a place for herself in the national politics of the Democratic Party. She and her brother came to Texas in 1833 on a colonizing project, and that is when she met William. She was a published author, under the pen name of Cora Montgomery, and was respected in literary circles.

Another book, *Eagle Pass or Life on the Border,* came out of her life on this segment of the Texas frontier. Jane Cazneau knew the problems of settling the arid lands; she recognized that the lack of rainfall and year-round streams and springs on the Texas side of the river would restrict settlement. What was needed, she felt, was industry based on the undeveloped mineral wealth of north-central Mexico. It could be successfully and profitably acquired, she wrote, because the Rio Grande offered a cheap way to transport it to market.[4] She also realized the importance of a navigable Rio Grande to the small towns springing up along it, including Eagle Pass, and she had little patience with the nay-sayers of the river's future. "Some wise-acres of our day are positively certain that the Rio Grande is not navigable," she wrote. "They speak of it by hearsay. It is rather much to say that the river is not navigable, when, of the . . . efforts to test this, every one was successful."

The results she portrayed were realistic: an ability to defeat the savage tribes, an ability to exploit the mineral riches of Coahuila and Chihuahua. She concluded that section of her book, "The last exploration was made by Lieutenants Smith and Mechler [*sic*] [who] went up from the mouth of the river to about one hundred miles above the mouth of the Pecos. . . .

Their report I have not seen, but their trip confirms the feasibility of the Bravo to light draught steamers."[5]

Had she read the report of Lieutenant W. T. Smith, Jane Cazneau would have had mixed feelings. Smith recommended $25,760 worth of improvements between Ringgold Barracks and Laredo and between Laredo and the first beginnings of Kingsbury's Falls. Such improvements would open the river to the largest steamers on it year-round. Although the falls could be opened, he felt that the economic development above them was too unsure to warrant the cost. Looking at the Mexican trade, Smith noted that the Rio Grande was slowly drawing trade from Veracruz and Tampico; in the future, he felt, it would draw the Chihuahua trade. For the time being, though, Kingsbury's Falls was the head of navigation. The savings to the military would pay the cost of improvements in one year. The military advantage in opposing the savage tribes was immense; settlers would be drawn to the irrigable lands between San Felipe Springs and the falls, providing future economic benefit. Lieutenant Smith sensed a bright future for the Rio Grande.[6]

The recommendations made by Lieutenant Smith should have been satisfying to Chapman. Colonel Joe Johnston of the Topographical Engineers wrote in his cover letter that opening the river made economic sense. The report and Johnston's recommendations were written in January 1851, too late to have any effect.

The *Major Babbitt* got back to Ringgold Barracks on August 11. Captain Love reported to Major Chapman two weeks later, and on September 5 the assistant quartermaster penned an eloquent report to General Jessup. It was published four times in the space of a month once it reached the East.[7] The fact that the report got such a wide circulation in so short a time is indicative of the interest and investment that northern financiers and businessmen had in the lower reaches of the Rio Grande.

In his opening paragraph, Major Chapman summed up a lengthy, well-thought-out appeal for continuing government service on the river; then he set out to prove the navigability of the Rio Grande: "Captain Love was instructed to carry [the *Major Babbitt*] to the highest attainable point on the Rio Grande. . . . He found this point at a distance of 967 miles above Ringgold Barracks, where his further progress in the keelboat was stopped by

the impassable falls. . . . Captain Love carried the skiff which accompanied his boat around the falls, launched her, and rowed her forty-seven
miles to other falls. . . . These are . . . about 150 by land below El Paso, 25
by land below the mouth of the Concho."[8]

Harry Love had reached the point predicted by Captain Easterly a year
earlier. Chapman and others were vindicated. The report went on to investigate improvements that needed to be made to make the river navigable
for small-class steamboats twelve months of the year. If large boats like the
Corvette were to be used, the channel would have to be widened in
places; they could use the river up to the falls, however, from June to November without making improvements. But Kingsbury's Falls had to be
improved. A channel for large steamboats would cost about three thousand
dollars; for keelboats and small-class steamboats, only five hundred dollars. The variance in the cost estimates of different observers can be at-
tributed to the stage of the river when it was tested and the completeness
of the improvements contemplated.

After discussing the falls, Chapman got down to the one thing he had
been after for two years: supplying El Paso by a combination of land and
water transportation. "From Kingsbury's falls up to the mouth of the San
Pedro or Devil's River . . . there is nothing to obstruct the navigation of the
river with steamboats of the largest class now running on the lower Rio
Grande. . . . The mouth of the Devil's River . . . is the head of steamboat
navigation. . . . Above this the Rio Grande runs between high mountains,
is deep, rapid, and narrow. It, however, could be navigated with some difficulty by keelboats to a point 65 miles above the 'Grand Indian Crossing' or
about 283 miles above the mouth of the Devil's River."

Chapman drew the obvious conclusion: if the channel at the falls were
cut, supplies for El Paso and Santa Fe could be brought by steamboat to
within three hundred miles of El Paso, meaning that the expensive land
route from Lavaca could be done away with. Chapman did not reinforce
his argument with comparative figures, but it cost the army about ninety-
two dollars and two months to get a barrel of flour to El Paso.[9] Chapman's
route would have cut about a month off the time and about sixty dollars off
the cost per barrel.[10]

Chapman offered complete proof of the Rio Grande's true potential as a

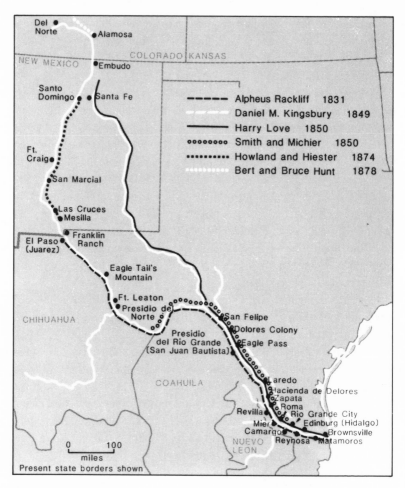

Explorations

carrier of steamboats and keelboats. Open the falls, the report said, and the Rio Grande will become a second Mississippi. But it was not to be. Charles Stillman was determined to make his steamboat line profitable. One way was to procure a lucrative government contract and use it to underwrite low civilian rates to drive out competition. That meant regulations pertaining to public advertisements and open bidding had to be surmounted. (Chapman's real estate dealings put him at a disadvantage.) If the river were opened up, there would be almost no way to eliminate other steamboat lines; increased settlement would make that inevitable. The river's fate was sealed. Climate precluded settlement. Private investment precluded competition, whether in the Mexican trade or by government contracts.

The boats designed by King almost guaranteed a profit, if they were operated properly. Stillman's knowledge of warehousing and forwarding came in handy at this point. While waiting for the new boats to arrive, O'Donnell oversaw the building of warehouses at Brazos Santiago and White Ranch, near the mouth of the river, the terminus of the operation. From the landing at White Ranch, both boats could go their separate money-making ways. The warehouses would store goods not immediately shippable, and the rental of space was another source of profit for the operation.

The new boats arrived about the time Captain Love returned from his exploration of the upper river. The big, beamy bar boat was named the *Grampus;* its smaller sister, the *Comanche.* The combination worked almost as well in fact as it had on paper.

Even before his glowing report of September 5, Chapman had begun to reverse his direction. For reasons that can only be surmised, he dispensed with the government bar boat *Anson* and turned her duties over to the *Grampus.* [11] One can only speculate about the reactions of the private owners on the river. Bodman and Clark's *Del Norte* was fully capable of towing those schooners and off-loading them; she was doing just that for private vessels. Other private owners, as well, were capable of performing the task. Quiet rumblings spread among many Brownsville businessmen. Among those disquieted by Chapman's action was E. B. Scarbourough, owner and editor of the *American Flag,* who knew many private owners and captains who wanted a shot at a government contract, including the master of the *Mentoria.* Stillman's company got the equivalent of one without even bidding or posting a performance bond. Chapman's halcyon days on the river were drawing to a close.

On November 28, 1850, Chapman wrote a report that contained his recommendations for navigation on the Rio Grande. It also included a list of private boats on the river, emphasizing the *Grampus* and the *Comanche.* The report has been lost, but from later letters it is clear that Chapman listed all other boats—private and government—as being woefully inadequate in comparison and as being in utter disrepair. He noted, therefore, that it would be in the public interest to give the two new boats government transportation contracts. Three months went by, and he had received no answer. On March 1, 1851, he queried General Jessup. He noted that he had not received a reply and that he would send a copy of his letter, if requested.

Chapman was no longer interested in opening the river. Never again would he broach the subject directly. His interests lay now in getting a contract for Kenedy and Company, and he put all of his efforts to work toward that end. Indications are that Chapman was asked to send a copy of the November 28 report. The next letter in the file concerned with navigation refers to the report as if Jessup were familiar with it, and Chapman's letter dated June 17, 1851, sounds as if it is an answer to Jessup's desire to know about the feasibility of contracting out supply and troop transportation. He felt that the expense involved in maintaining the "public boats" was too great. Chapman agreed with him, up to a point, but added that, all things considered, the government boats did the job cheaper than private boats could possibly do it, if the cost of maintenance was discounted. The *Corvette* was old, and even with a thorough overhaul she would be good for only eight or ten more months. Then she would need replacing at a cost of twelve thousand dollars. The *Mentoria* was in good condition. No mention was made of the *Major Brown;* she had disappeared from all records, her fate unknown.

Chapman then noted that if the army carried out its experiment of supplying the upper posts by land, the government boats then in use would be unnecessary. It is a flimsy acquiescence; boats would still be needed to supply Fort Brown and Ringgold Barracks. "Messrs. Kenedy and O'Donnell are the 'responsible and reliable' men and owners of the new boats 'Grampus' and 'Comanche' to whom reference was made in my letter of November 28th 1850—the prices named in this offer appear to be fair and reasonable, and as they own the only good boats on the Rio Grande, *they are the only persons with whom it would be judicious to make a contract.*"

The first step toward securing a contract without bidding had been taken. Friendship and loyalty meant much, especially in the risky ventures of real estate speculation and warehouse investment.

Once the wheels were set in motion, the result was inevitable, considering the business and government climate of the nineteenth century. Kenedy had to make a trip to Washington before Chapman was allowed to sign contracts,[12] and from events that transpired three years later, it is clear that Kenedy discussed more than contracts. But the contracts were finally signed.

On July 22, after discussing the probable income to be realized from selling the public boats, Chapman could not resist writing, "From Ringgold Barracks to Laredo, they are forwarded by wagons and Keel boats; from Laredo to Eagle Pass by wagons." In other words, Laredo had become a transient depot, much as had Ringgold Barracks. There was a system in place that was much cheaper than any land-bound transport system could ever be. In essence, Lieutenant Smith's recommendations for supplying forts McIntosh and Duncan were being followed. Apparently Chapman was still hoping that the difference in cost to the Quartermaster Department, when compared with the Kenedy and O'Donnell offer, would convince someone that public boats should be kept in service.

To get one barrel of any commodity from Brazos Santiago to Fort Brown cost $.40; from Brazos to Ringgold Barracks it was $1.25. The contract that was under consideration—and finally signed with minor changes—called for prices varying from $.50 to $1.00 per barrel to Fort Brown; thus, when the *Corvette* carried a thousand barrels of supplies to Fort Brown, it cost the government $400. When Kenedy and O'Donnell carried it, the costs could vary, depending on the commodity, from $500 to $1,000. Even assuming that every trip was at the minimum charge, the difference between government and private charges would have paid for a new *Corvette* in 120 trips—about a year or a year and a half. The prices charged did seem high, as Lieutenant Colonel W. G. Freeman, assistant adjutant general, pointed out in an inspection report.[13]

It was August 15, however, before Chapman felt in a strong enough position to broach the subject of awarding the contract without actually advertising for bids, and he was careful to justify such an action. First, the prices offered were the best that could be obtained; second, Kenedy and O'Donnell owned the only "safe" boats on the Rio Grande; third, it had been "generally understood" for some time that a contract would be offered, and no one had approached him about it; and fourth, he knew of no one who desired such a contract. (He was certainly aware of Captain Anderson's interest. After all, Anderson skippered the *Mentoria*—and Bodman and Clark had been talking about a contract since first being queried in 1848.) "For these reasons," Chapman added, "I did not deem it necessary, on the receipt of your letter of the 5th instant, to offer the contract for public advertisement." Then he wrote, "It, however, can still be done should you consider it in any way advisable." The final sentence freed him of responsibility and placed it in Washington. In subsequent memos from General Whiting in San Antonio and General Jessup to the War Department, the final sentence was not mentioned. Also, both wrote that "Chapman says" there was no one capable of fulfilling a contract, so that competitive bidding was unnecessary. Both—but Whiting especially—knew better.

It was January 5, 1852, while Kenedy was in Washington, before the contract could be gotten approved by the Washington bureaucracy, but the signing had to await Kenedy's return from Washington on February 10. The signing of the contract marked the end of competition for Kenedy and Company. The charges the government paid—coupled with the efficiency of their operation—underwrote low charges for nongovernment shipments with which the private boats could not compete. One by one they, like Bodman and Clark, sold their boats to the new company or took them to more favorable waters. The Rio Grande no longer offered its navigable bounty to any but the firm consisting of Stillman, Kenedy, King, Penny, and O'Donnell.

The tumult raised by these owners and captains and by Brownsville businessmen grew. Charles Stillman had a monopoly on trade, not only on the river below Roma, but at the Brazos Santiago as well. (Among those whose profits depended on the Brazos and the Mexican trade were Joseph San Román and James Grogan.) South Texas and interior Mexico were at Stillman's mercy. There was nothing his detractors could do except talk. In just two months, the talk was common enough in Brownsville that almost everyone was aware that the contract with Kenedy and Company had some kind of problem connected with ethics—especially when O'Donnell, highly respected and liked by all, withdrew from active participation in the company. The complaints were so general, in fact, that on April 8, 1852, President Fillmore was written the following letter.

I hope you will excuse this as I write to you about a good and faithful man. I mean Major Chapman, our Quartermaster. His enemies say that they are going to tell you that he speculates in land, and that he sells arms to the filibusterers, and that he helps to support Carvajal[14] as to make more freight for the steamboats by keeping soldiers on this river, and that he owns part of these steamboats that has the contract to carry government freight now, for it is very hard that such a good man should be complained about when he does his duty, and I hope you will not believe a word it is said. It is not true. The Major don't know I write this, but I am his friend and don't want to see such a good man envied and [slandered]. Even if he does speculate in the land where Ft. Brown is, it is better for the United States because he will not let his partners ask the U.S. too much for it.

I am respectfully sir, your obedient servant, Thomas P. Summerland

Summerland was repeating what he had heard. On April 6, Robert B. Kingsbury, a prominent Brownsville citizen and member of the Texas House of Representatives, wrote Congressman Volney Howard about conditions in Brownsville.

Great surprise and dissatisfaction has been created here in consequence of the Quarter Master General having contracted at an enormous rate with a Steamboat Company for the transportation of Government Freights. . . .

The principal stock holders in this Company are Major Chapman and Charly Stillman although they do not appear as interested in the boats. . . . Chapman so managed the deal that the government boats were not offered for sale until Captain Kenedy had gone to Washington and closed the deal with General Jessup. The company, it is understood, receive about double the rate that the contract would have been taken at provided there had been any competition.

I think it is a damned corrupt and unhealthy state of affairs.[15]

Congressman Howard took the matter up with the secretary of war, C. M. Conrad, who requested that Howard get him positive proof of Chapman's interest in Kenedy and Company. By the time the request got to Kingsbury, he had had second thoughts. In reply to the request, Kingsbury wrote Howard on May 12:

I did not wish to be understood that I knew positively that Maj. W. W. Chapman is a stockholder in the Steamship Company . . . but that report and very common belief existed here that such was the fact. . . .

I hope that my name is not used any further in connection with this affair. The masters of the Steamers are very clever men and friends of mine and perhaps would think very hard of me if they should know.

Comparing the tone of the first letter to that of the second, it is plain that Kingsbury had been talked to, perhaps by his "friends." However, he did include a series of questions that he felt needed answering. The most important of them was worded, "Was it not strange that no one except the members of this company should know that such contract was to be made? . . . [Chapman] knew well that there would be the most spirited competition for the contract—he well knew that the service could be performed at a lower rate."

Conrad acted as effectively as he could without outright proof of Chapman's part ownership of Kenedy and Company. Chapman was abruptly ordered to report to Colonel Tompkins at Eighth Department headquarters in San Antonio.[16] His days as overlord of the Rio Grande were ended. First Lieutenant J. P. Garesche of the 4th Artillery was named acting assistant quartermaster at Fort Brown and on the Rio Grande. Chapman, still the assistant quartermaster, could only react to events, not create them.

River-tides

Chapter 5

While Kenedy and Company were busy securing their government contract, the farmers of the upper reaches were busy siphoning off more and
more Rio Grande water. Since pre-Columbian times various agriculturalists
had used the Rio Grande in a manner that calls to mind the ancient Egyp-
tians. Every spring the river rose as the winter snows melted. As it rose,
water flowed into ditches and ran through them to encourage crops. Spanish and Mexican efforts were not much different. There was little need for
diversion dams or channel dams. Down in Chihuahua, where the banks
were not conducive to such a practice, stacks of rocks were placed in the
river to encourage its rising waters to flow into ditches. At El Paso (Juarez,
after the French intervention) a great canal, called the Mother Ditch, had
been dug by the early Spanish settlers. It supplied water to farms far from
the river.

After the Mexican War, when the local farmers were assured of more
dependable markets than they had known, irrigation expanded. Up in the
San Luis Valley of Colorado, where no irrigation had been practiced, live-
stock raisers began using Rio Grande waters for the first time as they
turned, slowly and grudgingly at first, to farming. When the railroads
came, irrigation expanded in a frenzy of development. Railroads brought
thousands of settlers to the valley; they took carloads of crops to market.
The two worked well together.

Irrigation ditches and projects increasingly drained the river, and for
every acre foot of water taken, a little more than half an acre foot failed to
reach the lower river. By the end of the first decade following the Mexican
War (1850–59), the developers of river prosperity were taking enough
water from it to lower the channel more than thirteen inches at Roma.[1]

Downriver, in 1853, a declining channel did not affect Kenedy and Company. They bought keelboats for use in seasonal low water and went about

the business of establishing sovereignty over the river; so booming did their business become that Captain Kenedy gave up command of the *Comanche* to Captain James B. Armstrong so that he could devote more time to the job of rivermaster. The pattern of Armstrong's replacing Kenedy on riverboats did not last. A dispute between them led to Armstrong's demotion to clerk;[2] animosity between Armstrong and Chapman, which had existed since Armstrong first came to the river,[3] led to either his dismissal or his resignation.

The original contract expired in February 1854; it was not renewed until July. Those letters from Summerland and Kingsbury had had their effect. The new contract cut rates by 30 to 50 percent, depending on the commodity to be freighted. (The company could afford the rate cuts; it had driven all competition from the river.) But the new contract, given without bids, was not satisfactory. A new secretary of war, reform-minded Jefferson Davis, may have asked that a new one be bid. Colonel Charles Thomas, Jessup's aide, may have prompted a new bid; Thomas disliked monopolies, feeling it "desirable" to break them down.[4] The Brownsville district congressman may have suggested a new contract, too. What exactly caused a new bid to be let will never be satisfactorily explained. But one was asked for, and on March 10, 1855, General Jessup wrote to Chapman, ordering him to advertise for competitive bids and to award the new contract to the low bidder, providing he was a "responsible" party.[5] Major Chapman, in Corpus Christi, the new headquarters of the Eighth Department, passed the orders on to Lieutenant Garesche at Fort Brown.

Garesche advertised for bids in Brownsville, Galveston, and New Orleans newspapers. Two bids were received. Kenedy and Company merely bid the same rates as in their 1854 contract. Captain James B. Armstrong, master and then clerk of the *Comanche,* made the other, and for each commodity to be transported, his bid rates were lower. The contract was his—if he proved to be a responsible party.

On June 15 Garesche wrote General Jessup, informing him that Armstrong had been awarded the contract. Concerning Armstrong's responsibility, the acting assistant quartermaster told the general that "Captain Armstrong holds himself prepared to give bond for the performance of this contract, should you require it. This security [is] Messrs. Grogan and San Román, who I have reason to believe to be two of the most substantial merchants on the frontier."[6]

Both San Román and Grogan had suffered from the high rates of the monopoly, and both welcomed the idea of setting up a competitive company; but San Román was the real drive behind the attempt to bring competition back to the river. With their support, Armstrong felt that he could oppose the monopoly and gain the contract. He did get it, but he found that bucking the monopoly was a different matter.

Kenedy's reaction was immediate. On June 10, five days before Garesche informed Jessup of the new contract, he penned a letter to Colonel Thomas, making three points upon which a basis for cancelling the Armstrong contract could be laid. First, he, King, and Stillman were the only "responsible" bidders, implying that Armstrong, Grogan, and San Román were not; second, boats and their serviceability should be considered; third, Armstrong must comply with every detail of the contract.

On June 21, Garesche wrote Jessup, reminding the general that the contract had been forwarded to him for action. He referred to Armstrong's excellent backing, and then asked that, if necessary, Armstrong be given some extra time to procure boats, since the time between the signing of the contract and its effective date, August 1, was rather brief for the procurement of boats. He also requested that all correspondence come through Major Tompkins at Eighth District headquarters.

Despite his caution, however, Lieutenant Garesche's letter gave reinforcement to Kenedy's. Armstrong's responsibility was strengthened, but the problem of boats and compliance was raised in Thomas's mind. Almost immediately upon receipt of the letter, July 12, Thomas answered Garesche's request. Armstrong would be required to post a performance bond. As to the problem of boats, Armstrong would have to have his own vessels in service—or make arrangements with other owners—by August 1. Otherwise, he would not be in compliance.

About July 1, however, the quartermaster general had sent a quick set of instructions to Chapman. Inquire into the matter, they said, and make sure that responsible parties are involved. A copy of Kenedy's letter was enclosed. Jessup's letter was short, terse, and to the point. Kenedy and Company, it implied, must be awarded the contract.

Garesche had not received Thomas's blunt letter, which, in effect, recognized Armstrong as the contractor, providing he had boats ready on the first day of August. Then he got a letter from Major Chapman, who had received Jessup's letter about July 5. Dated July 15, it reveals Chapman's agitated state of mind. "By order of the General [Percival Smith] commanding the Department of Texas," he wrote, "you will suspend all action in regard to the new contract until you receive instructions from him."

Garesche was further instructed to continue using Kenedy and Company boats for the transport of government goods and troops. In addition, Chapman claimed that the general wanted the answers to a series of questions that really had nothing to do with the contract: "You will report to me whether Mr. Armstrong is a responsible man and whether he is well prepared to carry his contracts into effect, and if he is himself the owner of property, if he is efficient and energetic, in fine, if he is as capable of performing the contract as satisfactorily to the government as M. Kenedy & Co. have theirs for the last four years.

"He [General Smith] directs you to report," the letter continues, "whether Mr. Armstrong is as responsible, as reliable, and as capable of carrying out his contract in good faith as the persons connected with the Company of M. Kenedy."

The general also wanted full information on Armstrong's boats—their seaworthiness, insurability, age, value, and running histories. Finally, the general wanted copies of the competing bids. In his fervor to create a situation so unfavorable to Armstrong as to void his contract, Chapman inadvertently demanded information on "whether Mr. Armstrong is as responsible, as reliable, and as capable of carrying out his contract in good faith as the persons with the company of M. Kenedy." That query laid open the old charges of collusion with M. Kenedy and Company.

Chapman sent a copy to Jessup, not Smith. It is probable that Chapman was acting on his own, with the approval of Jessup. The major's orders of March 10 included only the requirement that the contract be given to a responsible low bidder. All other questions raised after Armstrong got the contract can be traced to Kenedy's letter of June 10. Chapman's letter of

July 15 supports the idea of collusion between him and Kenedy—and Jessup.

If Chapman thought that his semitirade would have any effect on Garesche, he was right; the effect, however, was not what he might have expected. Chapman's tone made clear that Garesche was to find in favor of Kenedy. Garesche, though, was not one to be cowed. He replied, on July 24, that Armstrong was a thoroughly responsible, reliable man, having the reputation of being efficient, capable, and "one of the *best business men,* and one of the *most honest* on this frontier."

As to property, Armstrong owned none that Garesche was aware of, but he did have five thousand dollars of his own, and "he has had considerable sums advanced to him by merchants of Brownsville, as well as of Roma . . . and Rio Grande City. His credit stands very high in this community."

Garesche then drove home the blade. "I am bound to say that . . . I think Mr. Armstrong quite as responsible, as reliable, and as capable of carrying out his contract as either Capt. Kenedy or Capt. King; and rather more so than one or two persons whose names I have heard mentioned as connected with the company."

The lieutenant added that he did not intend to disparage King or Kenedy, but rather to show his estimation of O'Donnell, who had proposed to sell his interest in the steamboat line to Captain Armstrong for $8,000. (The sale fell through because of ill-feeling between Kenedy and Armstrong.)

As to the boats Armstrong proposed to put in use, the "outside" boat was the *Swan,* of Galveston, and the boat to make the upriver runs was the *Guadalupe,* recently in service on the Guadalupe River. He was not personally acquainted with them, but he did enclose a clipping from a Galveston newspaper that gave an indication of their cargo capacity. In addition, Garesche suggested that reports from the boats' New Orleans insurers and from government inspectors would reveal seaworthiness and suitability. Kenedy and Company did have a new boat, the *Ranchero,* which was built especially for upriver service. Of their other three boats, however, he had heard pretty much the same stories as of the *Swan,* and that there was "little to choose among them."

The lieutenant immediately wrote Armstrong, then in Galveston procuring his boats, about the suspension and advised him of the problems being encountered with Chapman. He also enclosed a copy of Chapman's letter.

Kenedy's and Chapman's efforts were succeeding; the suitability of boats was becoming more of an issue than the terms of the contract. The ability of Armstrong, or his backers, to perform reliably and capably would not become an issue in the forthcoming battle of Chapman (and Jessup), Kenedy, King, and Stillman to maintain monopoly. The issue was boats.

In late July, King made a trip to Corpus Christi to talk to Chapman. The conversation must not have been satisfactory, because on August 2 Kenedy took pen in hand to give more ammunition to Chapman for transmission to Jessup: ignore the suspension, ignore the *Swan*'s on-time arrival, ignore the proposed rates, bond had not been made, Kenedy's boats were better suited (an old ploy), and—finally—Kenedy and Company had a track record while Armstrong did not. Chapman wasted no time in transmitting the letter to Washington.

Armstrong, meanwhile, began to run his boats in competition with Kenedy and Company. His boats were able; the *Swan,* which he wrote could go anywhere there was four feet of water, ran from the Brazos to Brownsville (which Kenedy's outside boats could not ordinarily do) and the *Guadalupe* upriver to Camargo, Roma, and Mier. His boats charged less, too. The monopoly, as far as both Mexican and American river merchants were concerned, was dead.

Even with a comfortable river trade, Armstrong was not taking the affair of suspension lying down. On August 7, he wrote General Jessup, informing him that the terms of the contract had been met in full. He also enclosed a copy of Chapman's letter of July 15 to Garesche; more to the point, he enclosed a letter from the correspondence between Congressman Howard and Kingsbury. Armstrong, too, could play hardball.

Jessup immediately wrote Chapman, who sent an almost hysterical message to Garesche on August 20: "You will without delay report to this office if you furnished Mr. J. B. Armstrong with a copy of my letter to you dated July 15, 1855, relative to the contract for the transportation of public supplies on the Rio Grande, or if you allowed him to take a copy or if he obtained a copy with your knowledge, or if you know how he obtained a copy." Garesche's answer was equally harsh: "I, myself, furnished Capt. J. B. Armstrong with a copy of your letter, dated July 15, 1855."

What follows points to the conclusion that General Smith was not a party to the letter in question. For also on August 20, and in a more sub-dued tone, Chapman wrote another letter to the acting assistant quarter-master at Fort Brown, informing him that General Smith wished complete sworn statements from every member of M. Kenedy and Company as to who had been connected with it at any time.

Garesche went to work. He had King and Kenedy make sworn affidavits, as directed. The two partners swore that they, Stillman, Robert Penny, and O'Donnell were the only ones who had ever been connected with the company since its organization in February 1850.

Armstrong and his friends were not playing a game; they were serious about breaking the monopoly. On September 4, about a month after Armstrong wrote Jessup, a "petition" was received by G. Huffman in New Orleans. He promptly forwarded it to G. D. B. DeBow (editor of the *Demo-cratic Review*) in Washington. It was from a group of Brownsville citizens and was addressed to General Jessup. "It is rumored," the petition began, "that William W. Chapman, Major and Quarter Master of the U.S. Army is likely again to be stationed at Ft. Brown in his official capacity—in view of which the undersigned businessmen & citizens of the Lower Rio Grande—beg leave to remonstrate against the Said Chapman being again on this frontier in our vicinity." The missile continued,

Major Chapman . . . has been engaged in private speculations of an extensive char-acter, some of them believed to be connected with the Public Service—and many of them of a character to interfere seriously with private enterprise. The said Chap-man has arrayed himself with certain parties in this region, in the local questions which have divided our community & which have been attended with great bitter-ness & aggravated feelings—and that it is believed that Chapman has used the pat-ronage & influence of his office to the prejudice of private citizens, and has mani-fested undue partiality with honest competition for Govt. Service.

For these causes the said Chapman has made himself odious and obnoxious to a large class of our citizens.[7]

It is plain that not all citizens of the "Lower Rio Grande" were intimidated by Stillman or Kenedy and Company. Coupled with the letters of Summerland and Kingsbury, along with the furor being raised by Armstrong's suspended contract, one can read the specific charges that had been in preparation for three years and that had finally been completed. The signers of the petition were obviously ready to put up hard evidence, if they had to. They included some with the letter: documentation of Chapman's real estate speculation in 1850–52. Not specifically mentioned, but held in reserve, so to speak, was the fact that Chapman's warehouse had, somehow, become the United States Customhouse—at a profit. By September 7, Chapman had accumulated sixteen documents in connection with the contract, including the affidavits of ownership of Kenedy and Company. Blissfully unaware of the flank attack being mounted through the "petition," he sent them to General Smith. In the cover letter, Chapman requested that he not be required to make a decision concerning the contract: "The reasons why I prefer that either yourself or General Jessup should decide this matter will be found in the papers, particularly in the letter of Mr. Conrad's . . . to Mr. V. Howard, and Mr. Armstrong's to you, in which allusion is made to my connection with the company of M. Kenedy."

Chapman went on to refer to the charge as an "old slander" for which he had suffered enough. He blamed his transfer from Fort Brown to San Antonio on the slanders, a transfer made "unceremoniously" by the War Department, despite his five years of service at that post. He was somewhat bitter: "[The order] directing me to report to Col. Tompkins in San Antonio . . . was dated only 11 days after the date of Mr. Conrad's letter to Mr. Howard, and before there was time to 'ferret' out the truth of the report of Mr. Howard's political friend."

On September 8 Smith wrote Jessup, enclosing the sixteen documents. The general was puzzled. It is plain that he did not know of the letters Chapman had written "under instructions from the General commanding the Department of Texas." He could not understand what Conrad's letter or the affidavits of Kenedy and Company ownership had to do with the letting of the contract. He had personally gone to Brownsville to discover the sources of the slander and falsehoods against Chapman and had found that feeling was running tremendously high against both Chapman and

Kenedy and Company. That feeling seemed to underlie Armstrong's bidding, but he could not prove it. Smith felt that such animosity barred
Armstrong from getting the contract.

The same day, Chapman forwarded the documents and his letter to
Smith to General Jessup. Such actions by Chapman indicate that he was
more than careful to let Jessup know every detail of what was transpiring
concerning Kenedy and Company. It was a pattern he had been following
for four years, one of blending information due others with legitimate reports. It let Jessup know the state of affairs from Chapman's point of view.
In this letter, Chapman officially informed Jessup of the suspension of the
contract and the use of Kenedy and Company under the terms of the old
contract—five weeks after the fact.

Letters flew from Chapman, Armstrong, and Garesche to each other, to
Smith, and to Jessup. So disgusted did Lieutenant Garesche become at the
entire handling of the contract that he resigned as acting assistant quartermaster. He was reassigned to the Adjutant General's Office in Washington
and was promoted to captain. All other things aside—including personal
animosity between Armstrong and Chapman and the old charges against
the major—the entire question of whether Armstrong would get the contract reinstated revolved around the suitability of his boats. Armstrong
produced documented proof of their worthiness. Chapman countered with
hearsay dressed up as truth. Jessup suddenly became the man in the
middle.

Armstrong, realizing that the entire Quartermaster Department, from
Jessup down to Chapman, was more interested in awarding a contract to
Kenedy and Company than in competitive bidding, wrote the secretary of
war on November 14. His letter detailed, succinctly, the history of the affair; Armstrong enclosed his copies of correspondence, including those
given to him by Garesche, and documents relating to the condition of his
boats. He also pointed out that although his boats had been in service at
the Brazos and on the Rio Grande since August 1—thus fulfilling the requirements of the contract—Kenedy and Company boats still carried government freight.

On December 5, Davis referred Armstrong's letter to Jessup for action.
On December 13, Jessup answered that the only question involved was

Armstrong's responsibility and the condition of his boats. "These . . . satisfactorily ascertained, [Armstrong] should have been at once employed. From a careful perusal of the papers," he added, "I am not entirely satisfied that Mr. Armstrong's means are suitable and reliable; but at the same time I think Major Chapman has not taken proper measures to determine the fact."

On December 17 he wrote Chapman, instructing the assistant quartermaster to ascertain the "facts" about Armstrong's reliability and the suitability of his boats. He could do so by "employing competent persons" to give him the answers.

Chapman asked General Smith to order a Board of Officers convened to examine the issues raised by Jessup. Smith complied, and on March 19, 1856, the board convened at Brazos Santiago to inspect the *Swan;* the next day it met at Brownsville to inspect the *Guadalupe.* The board admitted that it knew nothing about steamboats or their requirements for operating on the routes called for by the contract. In order to inspect the *Swan,* it employed A. S. Ackley, captain of the schooner *Chrysolite,* and J. S. Russell, first officer of the government steamer *Nautilus.* Captain Butler, the insurance agent at Point Isabel, gave the Board of Officers government inspection certificates and the insurer's certificates as well. Getting someone to inspect the *Guadalupe* at Brownsville proved to be impossible. When the board went to Brownsville to inspect her, she was on an upriver trip, and the board had to wait for her arrival. When she finally pulled into her landing, no competent persons could be found to inspect her: everyone on the Brownsville waterfront was employed by either Armstrong or Kenedy. The board was forced to do its own inspection, admittedly an incompetent one, and to rely on its own judgments.

On March 23, 1856, the board determined—without evidence—that Armstrong was not responsible. It found that his boats were unsuitable and that there was no third boat to use if one of his two was wrecked or incapacitated. To give Armstrong a contract, they felt, would be a mistake.

The second finding was based primarily on the observations of the "competent persons" who inspected the *Swan:* she was a sidewheeler with narrow guards, thus presenting problems for off-loading (the same was true of Kenedy and Company's boats at the Brazos, but no mention was made of it); and, being built for river trade, she was not fit for the outside trip from Brazos to the river's mouth. (Government inspection reports and Captain Butler's insurance reports were ignored.) The board also overlooked her history. She had been an outside boat in the Galveston trade before coming to the Brazos. She had a strong history of performance.

As for the *Guadalupe,* the board also overlooked her government inspection and insurance report papers in making its decision. Board members relied on personal recognizance and were unsure of themselves and their findings. They merely noted that she had "apparently undergone many repairs." In addition, Armstrong owned no keelboats ("barges," the board called them) to make upriver trips if the river fell. (Such a contingency would have been unthought of five years earlier; irrigation upriver was taking a noticeable toll on the river.)

The board did append all government inspection and insurer's reports to its findings. Perhaps that is why no official action was ever taken on the report. It was not even released. No one except Chapman, Smith, and Jessup knew its contents until much later. Armstrong continued to operate his boats in successful competition with Kenedy and Company, whose boats continued to haul government supplies, but at rates that prohibited the company from temporary unprofitable civilian rates.

In late February—the month before the survey—Kenedy had made a special trip to Washington to see Jessup. With him he took a letter from Texas Senator Thomas Rusk and Congressman P. H. Bell. The letter primarily concerned his capability and responsibility as a government contractor and was written as a letter of introduction. With him, too, he had taken two due bills—one for $4,150, the other for $12,873.32.[8]

Chapman forwarded the board's report to Jessup. The general must have read it with care and a bit of consternation. There was great discrepancy between its recommendations and the official documents sent with it. Jessup had a problem to solve, and he tried to play Solomon. On June 4, 1856, he wrote the new acting assistant quartermaster at Fort Brown, Lieutenant W. E. Gill, who had also served on the Board of Officers: "You will forward the stores by either line which has a boat ready at the time, without waiting for, or showing favor to, one or the other of the owners. You will be careful to pursue a disinterested course in regard to the rival line of steamboats, so that neither party shall have any legitimate cause to complain of favoritism being shown to either."[9]

It is clear that Jessup was in an uncomfortable situation. It is equally clear that Armstrong should have been awarded the contract. He had met each challenge to his responsibility and his boats' suitability and had won. The general wrote Chapman the same day he wrote Gill, saying that no contract would be offered at "this time."

Jessup's decision gave Kenedy and Company all the advantage. Owning two more boats than Armstrong, they were much more likely to be in a position to secure government freight. If Armstrong were to compete for government transport, he would have to sacrifice his profitable civilian business.

In July King so arranged things that Chapman, who was already running some stock on King's land, became a bona fide Texas rancher. Gideon Lewis, an old friend of King's, owned an undivided half-interest in the Rincon de Santa Gertrudis Tract, which composed a goodly portion of the ranch at that time. When he died, intestate, his interest was to go on the auction block. All Chapman had to do, since King claimed that he could not be present, was make sure he was high bidder. In return, he received half of it. King meant to keep his ranch comfortably intact. The two partners signed a promissory note for the land, and Chapman was a member of an order of knighthood that still attracts followers.[10]

Even before Chapman became a Texas rancher, Joseph San Román was taking steps to remedy an unsatisfactory situation. Armstrong's procedures, administered through his guidance, had not succeeded in getting the suspension lifted. San Román sought out Stephen Powers. After gathering all of the papers, reports (except that of the Board of Officers), and testimony available on the river, he wrote DeBow on June 26. Powers asked the Washington editor to take the matter through all proper channels, beginning with Jessup. San Román was going to exact his pound of flesh from the Quartermaster Department and from Kenedy and Company. Powers set forth the facts of the case briefly yet forcefully. He was careful to give Jessup the benefit of any doubt he might have had as to the general's complicity in the matter, even blaming Chapman for the "subterfuge" question of Armstrong's ability to replace a boat if one failed—a question first raised by Jessup in his correspondence with Chapman. Powers repeatedly pointed out the wealth, ability, and reliability of San Román and the business community of the Rio Grande who composed the association that supported Armstrong. Jessup apparently turned down the appeal, making an issue of the dates Armstrong's boats arrived at the Brazos. Powers wrote DeBow on September 15, enclosing notorized affidavits of witnesses to the arrival time of the *Swan,* noting that "she was followed soon by the *Guadalupe* and other boats." He added, "Certain it is that very extraordinary measures were taken to keep [the contract] out of Armstrong's hands." Then, with no introductory warning, Powers set forth San Román's terms for settlement: "Mr. San Román instructs me to say that he wishes to press for damages for past [breaches] of the government and persist in demanding for compliance with the term of the contract, either for the unexpired time, or for the full term of two years from the time effect is given to the contract." Powers added, almost parenthetically, that San Román refused the terms offered by Jessup in his letter to Gill on June 4, 1856. DeBow made his appeal to Davis on October 8. An early decision was also requested. The secretary of war preferred not to be involved and apparently suggested an appeal directly to the Court of Claims. The appeal was immediately made.

James D. McPherson, deputy solicitor, was placed in charge of it, and he immediately went to work, taking a deposition from Captain Garesche. Then he began to look for a copy of Jessup's letter authorizing the bid and contract. It took two letters to get the copy.

Something happened in December 1856 or early January 1857 that caused a complete rupture between Jessup and Chapman. Jessup's next letter concerning Chapman reflects nervousness, at the very least. It was written on January 16, 1857, and was addressed to Colonel Cooper in the Adjutant General's Office. "I request that Major W. W. Chapman be ordered to report to the commander of the Department of the Pacific without waiting for [a replacement]." [11]

There is no prior basis for Jessup's action. It was sudden and uncharacteristic—especially when one considers the relationship that he and Chapman had maintained since April 1848. It must have been a powerful and sudden blow that forced the letter. The Adjutant General's Office gave Chapman his orders but modified Jessup's request so that the transfer was not to take effect until it was convenient for the Department of Texas. Chapman was still in Corpus Christi in February, overseeing the removal of government stores to San Antonio, once again the headquarters of the department.

According to Tom Lea—King's biographer—Chapman's reaction upon receiving his transfer orders was one of erratic behavior, out of keeping with his past record. Lea claims that the major rode almost immediately to King Ranch headquarters, some thirty or more miles away, looking for his partner. King was not there. The distraught Chapman accosted James Bryden. Babbling and almost incoherent, he told Bryden that he had been transferred to California, that he was to leave immediately. Chapman was giving his portion of the Rincon de Santa Gertrudis Tract back to King. He couldn't pay for it, he said (he was not expected to, if Lea's rendition of its acquisition is correct); he'd write about it; and he rode away.[12] Some doubt may be placed on the story, since Lea places the time as immediately following the partnership arrangement in July, not the following January or February, when Chapman's ride and statements would have had to have taken place.

Chapman never made it to California. He procured leave in New York, then was stationed in Massachusetts, then New York. All the while, Jessup was trying to place him in out-of-the-way outposts, but some power was keeping him close to Washington. He testified before the Court of Claims in 1858 and was transferred to Fort Monroe, Virginia, in early 1859. He died soon after.

Chapman was not the only participant in the contract game to hold a losing hand. Armstrong still had not heard the results of the Board of Officers survey of the year before. On February 4, he wrote Captain Garesche, "I have been kept in suspense by General Jessup since March last in relation to the results of the examination of the Board of Survey ordered by General Smith to examine into the condition of stmrs *Swan* and *Guada-*

lupe." He enclosed a copy of the letter that Jessup had written him the previous March concerning the board, a letter that really said nothing. Garesche was aware, of course, that DeBow was handling a claim for damages. Did he happen to have a copy of the letter of March 10, 1855? "If you could give me a copy of it you would confer a favor."

That is the last letter from Armstrong. He died sometime in 1857.[13]

Shoal Waters

Armstrong's death temporarily ended Joseph San Román's attempt to offer competition to Kenedy and Company. In his role as executor of Armstrong's estate, San Román sold the *Swan* and the *Guadalupe* to Kenedy, and he not only recovered his (and others') investments but provided some additional aid to the heirs.[1] On November 11, 1858, the Court of Claims finally made a decision. Armstrong had been wrongfully deprived of his contract. The $200,000 claim filed by his estate was reduced to slightly more than $17,000, the actual amount that Armstrong would have collected; and the case was closed on November 22, 1860. It would still be fifteen years or more until any money was collected; the Civil War interrupted matters before his heirs received their shares. In 1873 payment was authorized, but the amount was trimmed to slightly more than $13,000 by Congress.[2] The following year a special bill was passed so that a Confederate veteran and heir could receive his share.[3]

San Román got some measure of revenge, though. The Mexican government seized the *Swan*. She never made profits for Stillman and his cohorts.[4] It was a hollow revenge. Stillman maintained a stranglehold on the Mexican trade, and except for a flatboat trade from Mexican settlements all along the river, Kenedy and Company boats were the only ones available for civilian or military use. Yet, as is so often the case when triumph is achieved, trends were growing that held the seeds of collapse: the headwaters of the Rio Grande were increasingly being tapped by Colorado farmers in the San Luis Valley; the Mexican government was borrowing far beyond its ability to repay; and, to the north and east, abolition and states' rights were on a collision course. Had San Román and his associates been able to read the future as well as their account books, they might have found a way to keep Armstrong's boats in service. The whole story of navigation on the Great River would have been changed.

By 1860 the normal flow of the river was perceptibly down by thirteen inches, a suspected abolitionist was elected president of the United States, and the Mexican government's debts to European powers had grown beyond its ability to pay. France, Spain, and England were threatening to seize Mexican ports in order to collect duties and the monies owed them. The level of the river was not alarming; smuggling was even more profitable than anyone could have predicted; and, somehow, people expected things in the United States to work out. They did not. Texas seceded from the Union, over the objections of Governor Sam Houston. Having failed to keep Texas loyal to the Union, he and some Texas leaders urged a return to an independent status. They were overcome by a wave of emotion, and Texas joined the Confederate States of America in 1861.

It seemed as if Kenedy and Company were blessed by the gods. After the Union established its blockade of southern ports from Virginia to the tip of Texas, the company gained a monopoly on Confederate trade as effective as its hold on the Mexican trade, for the only port open to the Confederacy became a bedraggled Mexican village on the beach just south of the Rio Grande's entrance to the Gulf. Bagdad was its name and war profiteering its game. It had no dock facilities or harbor; it had no banks or warehouses. What it did have was a neutral flag and immunity from Union blockaders.

A "cotton road" was established. It trailed down by Corpus Christi and then to Brownsville, via King's ranch. After the Union took the ranch, the road moved west, leading to Laredo or to Eagle Pass. (When Union troops attempted to take Laredo in 1864, in order to interrupt the cotton trade, they were soundly trounced by a numerically inferior Confederate force under Colonel Santos Benavides of Laredo.) Once at Laredo or Eagle Pass, most of the cotton was taken by wagon down the south and west banks of the Rio Grande to Mier, Camargo, or Matamoros and Bagdad. A goodly portion of the cotton reaching Laredo was loaded on flatboats or, in high water, on steamers for the downriver trip. In 1865 one steamer failed to get downriver. She sank north of present-day Zapata after grounding on the shoal bar of an island (the same bar over which the *Major Brown* had to be pulled), with no loss of life. Her paddlewheel was found in the channel by Oscar Gutiérrez during the drought of the 1950s and was put on display at his restaurant in Zapata until Mrs. Sarita Kenedy East traded a cow and a calf for the remnant of one of her father's boats.[5] Folklore says it was a Kenedy and Company boat, but this is doubtful. There is no record of the company's ever having sent a boat beyond Mier.

Laredo folklore tells of another unfortunate riverboat incident in 1863. Having arrived at that city late in the season, the boat was forced to lay over and wait for the spring rise. She never made it downriver with her cotton. While hove-to at Zacate Creek, south of town, she was so vandalized by souvenir hunters that even her helm was taken.[6]

Ships by the hundreds languished in the trade winds off Bagdad and lightered their cargos ashore while bales of cotton were lightered to them. Kenedy and Company boats carried Confederate cotton down the river from Brownsville and Camargo and Mier and other river points, making as much profit from a single bale of cotton as from a whole cargo months earlier. Then, in 1863, the Union took Brownsville. To protect their boats from seizure, Kenedy and King placed them in Mexican registry under Mexican owners' names and continued in business. For safety's sake, they also established their residences in Matamoros. Business was booming; gold—the only currency they accepted—poured into their coffers. And, their boats being under a neutral flag, they even found profit in carrying cargos for the occupying Union forces. To show their true neutrality, after the French invaded Mexico and installed Maximilian on the throne, the company allowed its boats to carry cargos for both the French Imperialist government and the *juáristas,* who sought to reestablish constitutional government in Mexico.[7] And Stillman added to his wealth by sending shiploads of Confederate cotton to New York. Truly, the gods smiled on Kenedy, King, and Stillman.

They did not smile on Mexico. In 1862 the English, Spanish, and French moved in concert to seize Mexican Gulf ports. When the English and Spanish discovered that Napoleon III intended to use Mexico's default of debts to flout the Monroe Doctrine and to establish a new French Empire with Maximilian on the Mexican throne, they withdrew. Mexico was thrown into a cauldron of anarchy and warfare. Benito Juárez, the legally installed president of Mexico, took his office with him as he fled, vowing to drive the French from his country. Guerrilla bands, some patriotic, others bandits, took up the fight; the French and their Austrian allies undertook the task of making the new emperor secure on a stolen throne. Mexico lay prostrate before foreign invaders and native patriots. Once more, political disarray led to economic chaos.

On the river, individual Mexican citizens profited mightily from the American Civil War. Many sided with the Imperialists, a few with the Republicans—among them Antonio Canales, the erstwhile leader of the Republic of the Rio Grande. Much of the Matamoros business community, however, followed Maximilian. After all, French and Austrian troops provided protection and secured the cotton trade for their profit.

Inevitably, such a lucrative trade brought competition to the river. The Verlanders, Matamoros cotton factors, began operating vessels, and Edward Downey brought his *Alamo* to the Rio Grande at the urging of San Román.[8] Upriver, at San Ignacio, Blas Uribe gathered a fleet of *chalones*— keelboats with high stern sails—to carry cotton from Laredo to Matamoros. The boats floated down and were pulled up, assisted by the stern sails, for the Gulf trade winds blew consistently in an upriver direction.[9] And north of Laredo, rich deposits of high-grade coal were strip-mined and shipped to Matamoros by flatboat and keelboat.[10]

Other owners, their names unrecorded, also came to the Rio Grande in search of the profits to be made hauling contraband to two (or was it four?) governments. Times could not have been better. Two years after the war ended, times could not have been more bitter.

By 1864 the partners were looking forward to peace and a resumption of the Mexican trade. In 1865 Lee surrendered, the last battle of the war was fought near Brownsville (an empty Confederate victory), and the *juáristas* began pushing the French and their Austrian allies out of Mexico. Kenedy and Company and the Verlanders put local Brownsville shipbuilders to work. The company ordered the *Jerry Galvan;* W. R. Verlander had the *El Primero, Mamie,* and *Enterprise* built. Delivery on many of the boats was taken before oaths of allegiance to the Union were given or verified; the new vessels could not be documented until the oaths were administered and recorded in Washington. As a result, some never got documentation; by the time it could have been arranged, they were out of service (because of economic distress) and tied up at dockside. Many never saw service. They were sunk by a great hurricane in 1867.[11]

In August 1865 Kenedy and Company sold the *Antonia* and the *Eugenio* to the French, who converted them to gunboats to protect their lines, strung out from Bagdad to Matamoros. In September the *Señorita* was chartered to them.[12] At the same time the company bought the *Enterprise, El Primero,* and *Mamie* from the Verlanders and acquired the *Alamo* from San Román to keep competition off the river. Other owners were also bought out. Those who would not sell at the time did so later.

Immediately after the war, several Kenedy and Company boats were seized by the Union occupiers. The behind-the-scenes negotiations went unrecorded, but the boats were abruptly returned, then chartered by the Quartermaster Department. The reason for that action was given as expediency. The department claimed that it could not man the boats. Kenedy and Company, it said, could.[13] Kenedy, King, and Stillman were following their pattern: buy them out or drive them out, using government contracts to subsidize low civilian rates. Monopoly must be protected. The company girded itself for a post–Civil War boom that it expected to surpass the one that followed the Mexican War.

In Mexico a caravan of trade goods on its way from Matamoros to Monterrey under a large guard of French, Austrian, and Mexican Imperial troops was set upon by Cañales's guerrillas. The Imperial Mexican troops turned on their former allies. In the Battle of the Convoy, the French and Austrians were massacred almost to the man. The end of the French intervention and the execution of Maximilian were at hand. Benito Juárez was going to reestablish constitutional government in Mexico.

The expected postwar boom failed to materialize. It was 1867 before Juárez reclaimed his presidency, and so the first two years of peace on the east bank of the Rio Grande saw a continuing warfare in Mexico that tore that nation's economy apart. After Juárez resumed power, Mexico was destitute, with a huge demand for goods and contraband but no way to pay for either. Her mines would have to be redeveloped, her fields replowed and reseeded. There was not even the wherewithal for that task. In addition, hordes of young men were released from the military factions of both sides, men who could find no jobs or means of survival. A great many of those in northern Mexico turned to banditry—crossing the Rio Grande to steal cattle and other stock and to gain riches and revenge for the Texas

War and the Mexican War. Both banks of the Rio Grande became a battle-field, not of confronting armies but of small bands of raiders from Mexico confronting the very basis of the South Texas economy.

The result was a postwar depression. There was no trade on the river, except for the military need for transport and communication. Kenedy and Company tied up four boats at White Ranch: the *Antonia,* reacquired from the French; the *Enterprise;* the *El Primero;* and the *Camargo.* They sold others and put but one upriver boat in service. Then came disaster. In October 1867 a furious hurricane hurled itself at the mouth of the river. Bagdad was washed away, as were the facilities on Brazos Island so vital to the Mexican trade and to the river; Point Isabel was battered. The White Ranch warehouses and docks were blown away, and the four boats moored there were sunk, as were some of the boats tied up at Brownsville.

By the end of 1869, the San Luis Valley and New Mexico irrigationists were pulling enough water from the river to lower the channel by more than two feet at Roma. Snags began to appear where none had been before, and there were actually crossings where deep water had been the rule only five years earlier. Rivermen grumbled that the river was changing for the worse; they blamed nature, not the poaching far upriver. Mexico's progress from the distressing French intervention was negligible, and her economic condition, if anything, worse.

In 1866 Charles Stillman suffered a stroke that paralyzed his left arm and generally weakened him. He took his profits and went to New York to retire. He died ten years later. He kept some interests along the lower river but divested himself of any in the riverboat operation. Kenedy and Company was reorganized as King, Kenedy and Company. About the same time, the partners hired William Kelly, rivermaster for the Union forces, as their own rivermaster. A paucity of trade, however, left Kelly with almost no duties other than supervising the boat that carried military transport and supply. King and Kenedy took the huge profits they had realized in gold and began adding to land purchases up in northern Cameron County and in Nueces County, only to have their herds rustled and run off to the Las Cuevas headquarters of the west bank raiders. So powerful did the Mexican intruders become that in 1873 a group of 250 conducted a raid on Nuecestown, twelve miles from Corpus Christi. Texans were furious. Those on the lower river called for armed intervention, and the governor, Richard Coke, sent Captain L. H. McNelly to the river with the Frontier Battalion of the Texas Rangers.[14]

The United States government responded. The navy sent an *Alabama*-class gunboat, the *Rio Bravo*, to Brownsville to patrol the river—then, fearing an incident that might precipitate a war with Mexico (which the border residents fervently desired), forbade it to do so.[15] Her life on the river was short-lived. She blew a boiler and was removed from service.

As the Mexican trade dwindled and tottered, the two partners spent more and more time protecting their ranching interests, leaving Kelly to attend to the river. By 1874 King and Kenedy's propensity to maintain monopoly had gotten them in deeper trouble with the Brownsville merchants than in 1855. Even the representatives of Charles Stillman came to look upon them with a tinge of disfavor. The steamboating partners opposed a short-line railroad between Point Isabel and Brownsville, going so far as to secure a charter to build one so that no one could. When their inactivity caused the charter's revocation and another firm built the railroad, they brought suit against rail competition and rejoiced when a hurricane washed it away. Without Stillman to guide them in the business of making profit, they fell back on the only thing they knew: steamboat monopoly. When the railroad was rebuilt and put into service, it marked the end of highly profitable steamboat traffic from the Brazos to White Ranch and Brownsville. Rail service took over, leaving only the upriver boats operating for profit.

Finally, with the river dropping more each year—so much that the five-month high-water season had dwindled to about one month of good water and four of mediocre flow—they sold to William Kelly. From 1874 on, the story of lower-river navigation became his.

Ironically, one of the first things Kenedy and King did when they retired from steamboating was to join forces with Uriah Lott, the "little giant" of South Texas railroading, and the Dull brothers of Pittsburgh. Together they chartered the Corpus Christi, San Diego and Rio Grande Narrow Gauge Railway. They intended to build it into Laredo, but construction was stopped at San Diego in 1876. Perhaps one reason the two ranchers joined the project was a provision of Texas law that allotted sixteen sections (sixteen square miles) of public lands for each mile of railroad track laid. The

Corpus Christi, San Diego and Rio Grande Narrow Gauge laid fifty-three miles of track. It would be five years before the line would be completed to Laredo, and that under new ownership.

Eighteen seventy-four was a fateful year. The advent of the short-line rail link between Point Isabel and Brownsville created a new mold for the Mexican trade. It was no longer necessary to off-load at the Brazos to outside boats that in turn loaded their cargos onto upriver boats. Instead, those vessels with too deep a draft to get over the bar at the Brazos offloaded directly onto railcars in a specially constructed barge. Those that could make it over the bar unloaded at Point Isabel; no bar boats or lightering or outside boats were required. Once goods arrived in Brownsville by rail, they were distributed by upriver boats from Brownsville to Reynosa-Edinburg, Rio Grande City–Camargo, and Roma-Mier. They occasionally reached Guerrero, in May or June, but seldom got to Laredo.

By 1874 navigation in the upper reaches seemed to be ready to take its place in the economy of upper New Mexico. Irrigation and settlement had brought more businessmen to reap the new prosperity. The narrow-gauge Denver and Rio Grande Railway was winding its way down from Denver, stretching toward the Rio Grande under the able direction of A. C. Hunt, former territorial governor of Colorado, and William J. Palmer, who had brought the Kansas Pacific into Denver. There was a need for rail service brought on by increasing agricultural production; profits could also be made by founding new towns and enticing great numbers of settlers to take up lands along the railroad—lands that would tap the Rio Grande for crop-producing sustenance.

While southern Colorado and northern New Mexico waited for railroads, some decided to investigate the river. It might be usable, they thought. Two of those who sought to explore the navigability of the river were John Dare Howland, "an artist of no mean talent," and H. T. Hiester, "a photographic artist." The *Santa Fe Daily News* first told of their plans on August 14, 1874: "Recently . . . two adventurous spirits of Santa Fe, artists by trade, dragged a boat overland to Santo Domingo where they embarked on their voyage to Mesilla, when they proceed to their destination, Chihuahua, Mexico, by land again. Their vessel is of the common flat boat species, and their painting paraphernalia will load them down somewhat, but they can none-the-less be confident of succeeding in their attempt to prove the Rio Grande navigable."

Howland was well equipped for such a venture. He had worked for the American Fur Company after running away from Zanesville, Ohio, at fourteen; had tried his hand at mining; had been secretary of the Indian Peace Commission; and, in between, had studied art in Paris. After making his voyage down the Rio Grande, he would be in Mexico for five years as an artist for *Harper's* and then would study in Paris again before returning to Denver.[16] Little is known of photographic artist Hiester.

Their trip was a success. On September 23 the *Santa Fe Daily New Mexican* carried the complete story of the voyage: "A boat of four tons burden was built, hauled by wagon to Santo Domingo, launched in the sparkling waters of the Rio Grande. . . , and christened the 'McGuffin.' On the 6th of August the 'McGuffin' with a cargo of four thousand pounds consisting principally of artists' materials & provisions, including a camera for taking stereoscopic views, was pushed out from the rocky bank at Santo Domingo. . . . That day they accomplished forty miles of river, passing the towns of San Felipe, Algodones, and Sandia, and at night arrived at Bernalillo."

Below Bernalillo, the two intrepid artists encountered their first serious obstacle: a wide, shallow river blocked by a sandbar. They were forced to lighten the *McGuffin's* load in order to get over it, then to reload. From that point to below San Marcial, at Fort Craig, they encountered few problems. The artists stopped at many of the towns along the way, painting and photographing local architecture and scenery. Eight miles below Fort Craig, "the 'McGuffin' plunged into a great canyon formed by the precipitous lofty walls of the mountain ranges on either side; here the pent-up waters rushed and foamed; in a distance of thirty miles, ten distinct rapids were passed."

The only serious obstacle before them was the "great cataract," which, they had been told, created a waterfall of fifteen feet. When they got to within four hundred feet of it, they landed. After inspecting the falls, which proved to be more of a steep, precipitous rapid with fast currents and dangerous rocks through its course, they unloaded the boat and got her over them safely; then, after reloading, they continued their journey. They made

Bruce and Bert Hunt's steamboat at Alamosa, Colorado. Note the upright boiler
and the shape of the hull—two reasons why it was unsuccessful. A paddlewheel
should have been placed astern. Courtesy Colorado Historical Society.

a triumphant landing at Mesilla. The *Daily New Mexican* was enthusiastic
about the possibilities that the *McGuffin's* trip downriver presented: "The
'McGuffin' is the first boat that has ever made this voyage, it has been several times attempted without success. Messrs. Howland and Hiester have
demonstrated that the Rio Grande can be navigated in time of low water.
They are of opinion that during the three or four months in each year when
the water is high, small stern wheel steamers can ply between any points
from Santo Domingo to Mesilla. There is no difficulty whatever in finding
the channel."[17]

As navigation on the lower river was declining, it seemed as though
upper river settlement might support riverboats and trade. It was a strange
standoff.

By 1878 the Denver and Rio Grande had reached—and founded— Alamosa, Colorado. The two teenage sons of Governor Hunt, fourteen-year-
old Bert and seventeen-year-old Bruce, determined that a barge line between Alamosa and Del Norte might earn some profits. They converted a

large sixteen- or eighteen-foot boat to propeller-driven steam, using a tall upright boiler that made her top-heavy. Their ignorance about shallow streams worked against them, for they should have provided the towboat with a stern paddlewheel and a horizontal boiler. On her maiden test voyage, her propeller struck a submerged rock; she turned over, and her boiler exploded. The boys were not hurt, but they abandoned the project.[18]

The boys had had the right idea. The only way riverboats could compete with rail was either to carry freight from the railhead to settled points not served by rail or to tow barges loaded with cargo that did not have to get somewhere in a hurry at higher rail rates. The weakness of the boys' attempt lay in their boat, which was designed primarily for rowing and fishing.

By the 1880s navigable streams had lost their lure, except for the romantic and the nostalgic. No longer did they represent national power through industry and commerce. They represented agricultural power through irrigation. An era was ending.

Downriver, navigation was fading, too. When William Kelly bought out King, Kenedy and Company in 1874, he had bought twelve outside boats and four for upriver use. By 1876 the outside boats were no longer needed; the upriver boats began to discover snags and shoals. Kelly designed and ordered a new class of riverboat in St. Louis: small, shallow-draft (about fifteen inches, loaded), and narrow-beamed. She followed the river trade up to Mier until 1902, when a combination of railroads and a falling river beached her except for occasional unscheduled trips. Her method of navigating a now shallow, narrow, twisting river was unique.

It often happened that as the *Bessie* came to a bend, the wind would push her stern about in a grand arc until the bow was wedged into the bank; then she would float free and sail on downstream stern first. At another bend, a chance came to right matters, . . . let the leading stern take the bank, and the breeze and the current brought the bow around until [she] sailed once more like a proper ship, pointing forward. The evolution was performed over and over, . . . and so she waltzed all the way [from Ringgold Barracks to Brownsville].[19]

Mexico's volatile political and economic condition could not last. About the same time that Kelly bought his steamboat company, General Porfirio

The *Bessie* at dockside. Activity on the boat and ashore indicates that the photograph was taken in about 1902, the year the *Bessie* made her last scheduled trip. Courtesy Hidalgo County Historical Museum.

Díaz, a hero of the republic during the French intervention, began a revolution aimed at finally establishing Centralist dominance and economic prosperity. His revolution succeeded; in 1876 Díaz became the dictator of Mexico. He immediately set about controlling the border intrusions. More important, he brought political stability—though at the cost of freedom and liberty for Mexico—and a fledgling economic rebirth to the Mexican Rio Grande.

Matamoros and Brownsville once again began to burgeon with foreign companies and shipping. Mexican produce, from both her mines and her fields, began to flow downriver to find its way to foreign markets.[20] As many as forty large steamers, and many more smaller ones, loaded at Brazos every month, and William Kelly's few remaining boats were kept busy making profits. Goods poured down the river by flatboat and by his steamers. Good times were back on the lower Rio Grande, as shallow and treacherous as she had become. But good times were not to last forever.

In 1881 the Palmer and Sullivan Syndicate completed a narrow-gauge railroad from the interior of Mexico into Laredo. They also bought the Corpus Christi, San Diego and Rio Grande Narrow Gauge from its builders, renamed it the Texas-Mexican Railway, and completed it to Laredo. The first passenger train from Corpus Christi to Laredo carried all the political, business, and ranching dignitaries from communities along the way, and its water coolers were filled with champagne. The rail link from interior Mexico to Corpus Christi doomed Matamoros and Brownsville. They were downriver, out of the way, and isolated. Laredo became the center of the Mexican trade and Corpus Christi its port.

Frank C. Pierce, who had come to the river as a crewman on the *Rio Bravo,* wrote of the consequences of the Palmer and Sullivan narrow-gauge railroad: "Prior to 1882, the Gulf of Mexico off Brazos de Santiago and the mouth of the Rio Grande was constantly speckled with large and small steamships from all points of the globe. . . . [But from 1882 to 1904] little was known of this historic country, though occasionally in the daily press of the State one would read "The Steamship Manteo" or "The Tugboat Luzon" had just arrived from Brazos. These two light draught [coastal] steamers supplied the Valley with its all."[21]

Trade had stagnated. Brownsville and Matamoros, once the focal point of the Mexican trade, became cut off, no longer important to profit-seeking shippers and traders. Not even the completion of a spur of the Mexican National Railway from Monterrey to Matamoros helped. The superior port facilities of Corpus Christi made Laredo the center of the Mexican trade. The *Luzon* and the *Manteo* coasted to Corpus Christi or to Indianola or to Galveston, picking up supplies for the river towns. Kelly's little riverboat took some cargo upriver, but not much. She brought back less.

With a railhead at Laredo, one might have expected a river trade to develop between Laredo and the downriver towns. Low-cost water transportation would seem to indicate such a necessity. But for thirty years the lower river had been geared to the Mexican trade; as a result, local growth and industry had been neglected, if not discouraged. There was no broader base than local need; the river towns had little population, except for Brownsville and Matamoros, and there was virtually no industry other than stock-raising. Local need, however, should have produced a trade down-

river from Laredo. Other factors than population and industry and railroads stunted navigation on the Rio Grande.

In 1902 the narrow-gauge tracks that ran from interior Mexico to Corpus
Christi were widened to standard gauge; a Mexican railway was built from
the interior through the Mexican river towns, reaching Matamoros in 1904.
Some trade revived as a result, but the river trade died, despite the fact that
some trade should have been engendered between Laredo and the downriver Mexican railhead. Some revival of river trade from Camargo to Brownsville should have emerged, but changes were taking place in the river; the
Bessie made her last trip when the Mexican railroad reached Matamoros.

An industrial river trade did survive at Laredo, however. In the 1870s the
rich upriver coal deposits were worked commercially once again. The coal
was placed in steam barges for shipment downriver and, when the railroads came, for shipment to the railhead. The barge shipments continued,
even after the Rio Grande and Eagle Pass Railroad was built to the mines,
but were discontinued sometime after 1890. A changing river, getting ever
shallower and more dangerous, contributed to the decision to shift to rail.
In addition, steam barges downriver, cheaper than the railroad and more
efficient, became empty barges upstream, which negated the advantage.[22]
There is some indication that a small steamer, name unknown, occasionally visited Laredo. When the international boundary commissioners were
on a survey-deposition trip in 1894, they went to Laredo to charter the
"small steamship." Before it could arrive, however, they were called to San
Antonio. The steamer traffic, because of a shallowing river, would have
had to cease soon after 1894.

About the turn of the century, agriculturalists and irrigationists began to
invade the lower valley. John Closner was the parade marshal, so to speak.
He called Wisconsin home but came to the Rio Grande from Mexico,
where he helped build one of Jay Gould's railroads. In 1883 he showed up
with his family and with only fifteen dollars in his pocket. He drove the
stage to Peña Station, for a while, then to Brownsville. He moved to
Hidalgo County to be near the center of his run and was made a deputy
sheriff in 1884. In 1889 he became sheriff. All this time, he was busy buying
up land for twenty-five cents an acre, accumulating a great deal of it. He

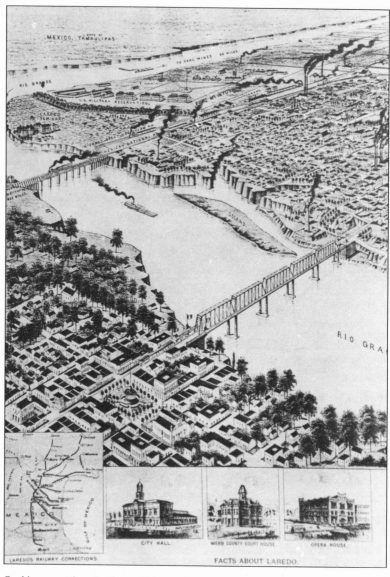

Coal barges at Laredo, from a lithograph map of Laredo, 1890. Courtesy Laredo
Public Library.

established a plantation downriver from Edinburg and built irrigation works to water its fields. One of his pet projects was growing sugarcane, but he was especially dedicated to developing the resources of the lower Rio Grande and bringing in settlers. To the visionaries of the late nineteenth and early twentieth centuries, rivers meant irrigation, not navigation.[23]

The lower-river farmers would find a river with a meandering channel and ill-defined banks, subject to sudden and destructive flooding. For centuries the first rush of the spring flood had cratered banks, shifted the bed, and remarked the river's course below the San Juan. Above that tributary, although changes took place, they were neither as drastic nor as shifting. Shortly after the American Civil War, things began to change. Spring flood surges were less damaging; susceptibility to sudden, unexpected flooding increased. As tropical storms and hurricanes blew in from the Gulf or battered the Rio Grande watershed in the western mountains, sudden flood caused havoc. Even where the river flowed through mountains and canyons, its course changed. Landowners became confused about whether their fields were in Mexico or Texas; legal jurisdictions became entangled in questions of which bank of the river was really Texas or Mexico.

The changes in river behavior could be traced to two sources: the denuding of upstream watershed timber by new settlers and the lack of a consistent flow in the river. After the new settlers had cut off the timber, especially in the lower elevations of upper New Mexico and southern Colorado, snow no longer remained all winter long, building a pack that would send down first a spring flood, then maintain a high river for five months or so. Instead, melting snow trickled down and fed the river, cutting the amount of water for summer flow and causing a winter runoff that had been unknown in times past. Coupled with an increasingly massive use of declining flood waters by irrigationists, the river ran increasingly lower as upriver waters were sucked up. A lower river meant that in the arid, hot climate of the Rio Grande, banks and flood plain were subject to drying out, cracking, and wind erosion. When the river rushed with unperiodic flood, the dry weather effects allowed surging waters to create more havoc than had ever been produced in pre–Civil War times.

Mexico and the United States thought about it and talked about it. In

1884 they signed a treaty that defined the problem but in no way solved it. Normal erosion and similar natural changes, the treaty said, were recognized as inevitable when determining the boundary. Changes in riverbed, though, required consultation as to where the boundary really was.

The water takers and the timber grabbers had created most of the problem. Without its consistent summer flow, the river could not cope with the whims of nature's summer storms, whether in the Gulf or in the Pacific. And when unusually heavy snowpacks accumulated in the high mountains that fed her headwaters, the Rio Grande could not receive them with the same facility as in the past. Civilization, so named by its practitioners, was creating unnatural problems.

Navigation was just about over. El Rio Grande or Bravo del Norte never became the harbinger of settlement and prosperity. Political anarchy, economic chaos, and irrigation took their toll on navigable progress.

In the end, it was irrigation that caused the collapse of navigation. After the railroads came, a sufficient amount of trade could and should have developed between Laredo and downriver points. Shoal water created by the upriver irrigationists prevented it. Eventually, none of the upper waters reached the Big Bend. The Great River, from Presidio del Norte to the Gulf, depended upon the Conchos to keep her bed wet. The Rio Grande described by Santa María and Green and Egerton and the United States Army ceased to exist.

Elephant Butte Dam saw to that.

Elephant Butte

Chapter 7

Both navigation and the international boundary were victims of irrigation in the San Luis Valley and upper New Mexico. Neither the United States nor Mexico was particularly interested in navigating the Rio Grande; boating, trade, and commerce on rivers had lost their power to create dreams. Both nations, however, were deeply concerned about the boundary problem, defining it in the Treaty of 1884. In 1889 a treaty was signed that created the International Boundary Commission. The commission was to investigate land and jurisdictional problems produced by the erratic Rio Grande, mark the true boundary as defined by the joint survey of 1852/53, and maintain its markers.[1] The first United States commissioner was Brevet Brigadier General Anson Mills, retired, of El Paso.

Then new and potentially expensive victims of upriver irrigation appeared: Mexican citizens claiming damages because that irrigation deprived them of water to which they were entitled by prior right. The El Paso Valley, even before the Spanish, had depended on the Rio Grande for its crop sustenance. Most of the valley irrigators were on the west bank, in Mexico. Fields were watered via a long canal, named the Mother Ditch by the Spanish, that took its waters from the Rio Grande and distributed them to farmers. On the east bank, waters were taken directly from the Rio Grande as it rose, flowing into irrigation ditches. So it had been for centuries.

But as the 1870s and 1880s stretched on, something changed: each year less flow entered the Mother Ditch or the downstream ditches on the east bank. Slowly, at first, fields began to die and orchards to dry up. The Mexican farmers of Chihuahua in what came to be known as the Juarez Valley suffered tremendous losses. The Texans did, too. What had been a highly productive agricultural region was slowly returning to the desert from which it had been wrenched. The Mexican minister in Washington, M. Romero, wrote secretary of state Richard Olney in 1897 that "[in the Juarez Valley] the loss of the public wealth in the last ten years [has been]

$22,840,000 and that of private individuals $12,845,000, amounting to a total of $35,685,000. . . . The government of the United States, and especially the State of Colorado, have obtained great advantages through the use of the waters in Colorado; the Federal government has been able to sell millions of acres of lands which are irrigated by the waters of the Rio Bravo del Norte and its tributaries."[2]

Romero went on to point out that while the population of the Juarez Valley had suffered an 80 percent decrease, the population of Colorado had increased threefold. Even the United States Congress got concerned with the problem. In 1890 it passed a joint resolution asking the president to negotiate with Mexico as to those claims—claims engendered by the San Luis Valley and upper New Mexico farmers. (The resolution was concerned not only with Mexican claims, but with the claims of Americans, too.)

There was a fourth victim. As railroads brought settlers to central and southern New Mexico, a clamor began around Las Cruces and Mesilla for more water. Upriver irrigation was depriving these newcomers of productive fields. A simple solution to their problem seemed to be a dam capable of holding back most of the unappropriated waters—the spring rise, which irrigated the few Mexican fields still in production and provided what remained of seasonal high water far downriver. An English-financed company, headed by Dr. Nathan Boyd of Las Cruces, innocently pronounced its intention to construct a dam at Elephant Butte, 125 miles above El Paso, to fulfill those desires.

And so a four-way fight for control of Rio Grande waters was created. The navigators downriver were innocent of their involvement; the Mexican claimants were partial creators; the International Boundary Commission got involved through treaty obligations; and the Rio Grande Dam and Irrigation Company precipitated it. A drama unfolded that would result in the lower Rio Grande's being totally deprived of upstream waters.

When Boyd announced his company's plans, the resulting outcry was deafening. Mexico took umbrage; El Paso demanded that the dam be built there to provide water to both sides of the river. One of the instigators of the El Paso plan was boundary commissioner Mills. He probably had dual motives. As a commissioner, he had certain responsibilities that would

Elephant Butte

have been easier to meet if the proposed dam were controlled by the government, which it would have to be to serve as both a controller of boundaries and a water provider. As a leading citizen of El Paso, he felt that if there were to be a dam, it belonged in his city. Mexico approved of the El Paso dam but disapproved of Elephant Butte. The former meant water; the latter, deprivation. In addition, a dam to control river flow would enhance the settlement of boundary problems.

The downstream river boatmen were virtually unconcerned. Boyd prepared to trap the river for profit and crops. The Rio Grande Dam and Irrigation Company hired engineers who, after intense surveys and planning, took their designs, plans, and plats to he secretary of the interior. The secretary, who had jurisdiction because New Mexico was a territory, not a state, approved all. The company immediately began to build sluices to carry the river while the dam was constructed and invested more than $150,000 in a downstream wing dam and canal system.

Mexico was moved to action. On March 21, 1895, the Mexican minister in Washington handed a note of protest to secretary of state Olney: "The Government of Mexico thinks that according to the Treaty of Guadalupe-Hidalgo of February 2, 1848, the inhabitants of one country cannot, without the consent of the other, build any works that obstruct or impede navigation on international rivers, and nothing could impede it more absolutely than works which completely turn aside the waters of those rivers."[3]

For proof of navigability of the upper Rio Grande, the minister might have cited the State of Chihuahua's report of 1834 or even the trip of the *McGuffin*. Instead, Minister Romero referred to the report of September 5, 1850, written by Major W. W. Chapman: "It appears that Captain Love, United States Army, ascended it [the Rio Grande] with several boats, reaching a point several kilometers above the Paso del Norte, which shows it was navigable at that time."

Captain Love did not ascend that far (see Chapter 4), but that was beside the point. Mexico was pressing the Treaty of Guadalupe-Hidalgo, which made *Las Siete Partidas*, the Seven Parts of Spanish law, applicable in territories ceded to the United States after the Mexican War. Under those provisions, obstruction of navigable streams was forbidden, and all streams were defined by them as navigable.[4] Had Mexico continued to press the treaty, action would probably have been taken to dismantle many of the irrigation projects of the San Luis Valley and upper New Mexico. But Mexico had no intention of such action. Her sole intent was, it seems, to see to it that water was made available to the Mother Ditch.

Attorney general Harmon ruled against the claim made by the note, but

Olney disagreed. The cabinet's sense was that the Rio Grande was a navigable stream, as defined in the Treaty of Guadalupe-Hidalgo. Under Anglo-Saxon usage, a navigable stream, to be so in law, must be so in fact. The Mexican minister had mistakenly cited Love's expedition as proof of this. Mexico was coming at the Elephant Butte dam project from two legal directions.

Mexico got action. The secretary of the interior immediately placed an embargo on further construction at Elephant Butte; the secretary of war, responsible for navigable streams, brought suit to prevent the construction of the dam. Commissioner Mills was familiar with navigation on the lower river. In September 1894 he and the Mexican boundary commissioner had been on the lower river, taking claims depositions and supervising the correction of boundary markers. The most devastating flood since the hurricane of 1867 had struck the lower river, creating chaos on the river's banks and, in places, destroying them. The commissioners went to Laredo, hoping to charter a small steamer to examine the banks as they went downstream. No steamer was there, and they found it necessary to go to San Antonio before one would arrive. From San Antonio they went to Camargo, rented the town ferry to use as a flatboat, and floated downriver for sixteen days, stopping where necessary to take testimony and to allow the engineers, among them W. W. Follett, to remark the banks. At last they received a telegram: Camargo needed her ferry back. They placed the flatboat aboard the steamer *Bessie,* which was on her way to Camargo.[5] To General Anson Mills, the Mexican claim was real.

In 1896 the boundary commissioners of the two countries asked that before claims were decided and boundary problems permanently solved, a means of controlling the erratic Rio Grande be agreed on. In support of the decision, Mills sent Follett and other engineers to the San Luis Valley, where they were to begin a detailed examination of the river from Del Norte to El Paso. When Follett turned in his report, he wrote: "This study was made for the purpose of investigating the claim of the Mexican Government that the people of the United States have taken from the inhabitants of Mexico water which was theirs by ancient right of prior appropriation. It also extends to the probability of there being a water supply sufficient to successfully serve a reservoir at El Paso, the construction of which by the United States is suggested as a recompense to the Mexicans for their alleged loss of water."[6]

It was an exhaustive study, covering tributaries, watershed areas, and the increase of irrigation from the San Luis Valley to El Paso. There would be sufficient water available, Follett said, to support the proposed international dam. (See Appendix 2.)

The 1896 resolution of the joint commissioners, along with the results of Follett's study, led to a draft treaty in 1897 that called for the United States to assume full control of the Rio Grande—including that portion of the river from its headwaters to the point at which it became the boundary. The treaty also called for the equitable distribution of those waters, including the waters to which Mexico was entitled.[7] Had the treaty been adopted, it is conceivable that all irrigation ditches and projects in the San Luis Valley and those built in New Mexico following the Mexican War would have come under government control, a thought that farmers found discomforting.

Before it could be acted upon, though, the Elephant Butte lawsuit brought international cooperation and amity to a halt. In its suit against the Rio Grande Dam and Irrigation Company, the government maintained that the Rio Grande was truly a navigable stream, in fact as well as in law, and that the construction of the Elephant Butte dam, taking all unappropriated waters, would seriously interfere with that navigation. Boyd's company claimed that the construction of its dam and the impounding of waters could not possibly interfere with navigation, since there was none. Boyd won in District Court, and the government appealed. Finally, the Supreme Court sent the case back to the Third District for retrial; the government conceded that the river was not (or no longer was) navigable in the upper reaches and pointed to downstream boating. It made no mention of the treaty obligations; to have done so would have been to return the river to its 1848 status.

The retrial was heard in the Third Federal District Court of the Territory of New Mexico in 1899. All of this took time, of course, and as the suit was winding its way back to the New Mexico courtroom, the parties involved became increasingly anxious. Both the Mexican and United States governments seemed determined to halt Elephant Butte, and the United States seemed determined to take control of the Rio Grande.

Thus battle lines were drawn: Coloradoans and New Mexicans maintained that their geographic position entitled them to all the water they wanted, even if downriver users got a dry bed. Texans and *chihuahuenses* proclaimed their prior-use doctrine. Both sides demurred from even mentioning the Spanish doctrine of riparian rights, which stated that in time of shortage, "all should suffer equally." It was a doctrine that would have diminished the waters available to all—and perhaps improved the navigable river.

By the time the suit came to retrial, the El Paso international dam loomed as a practical, viable alternative to the privately owned one proposed at Elephant Butte. The draft Treaty of 1897 was awaiting court results.

Coloradoans were intensely interested in the outcome of the second trial. All that had passed since Dr. Boyd first proposed his dam and irrigation project proved to them that the government was "out to get them." The *Denver Times* sent a reporter to Las Cruces to cover the trial. It ran his story on December 17, 1899:

> Some Very Valuable Testimony Heard from on the
> Last Day Showing Flood Waters of the Upper Rio Grande
> are Lost Before Reaching Head of Navigation

Las Cruces, N.M. Dec. 16 (Special). By far the most valuable and interesting testimony of the trial of the Elephant Butte dam case, at least from the standpoint of the defense, was introduced today by the experts and engineers and demonstrated pretty conclusively the theory of the defense that the flood waters of the upper Rio Grande are absorbed and lost before reaching the alleged head of navigation, and secondly that the lower Rio Grande does not depend on this section of the river for its water supply.

Witnesses were paraded before the court, witnesses from Laredo who testified that in their lifetimes, the river had changed little. (None who had experienced the river on coal-carrying steam barges appeared.) Expert engineers and hydrologists testified that the waters of the upper river could not possibly reach and affect the lower Rio Grande. The government was surprised by the tactic. Proponents of the dam were admitting that the river was "allegedly navigable" below Roma but that Colorado and New Mexico water never got that far, so the case was moot. The government, it seemed, was caught with its expectations down.

The government lost, and the appeals process began all over again. The appeals court held that there were no grounds for claiming error—that the government should have been ready to disprove the water-flow allegations, and that since it was not, they must be true.[8] The Supreme Court disagreed with the reasoning and again sent the case back to the Third District. The Justice Department was determined to be ready. International Boundary Commission engineers were told to determine just how much water from the San Luis Valley and upper New Mexico reached the head of navigation.

Meanwhile, hearings were going on in Congress concerning the proposed international dam at El Paso. Coloradoans and New Mexicans were determined to put a stop to such nonsense, and they brought all of their feelings and theories to Washington with them.

The subcommittee appointed to take testimony met on May 25, 1900.[9] The hearings were on H.R. 9710, which provided for the international dam at El Paso and the equitable distribution of Rio Grande waters to Mexico; interestingly, the United States would bear the whole cost, in lieu of paying damages to Mexico and to Mexican citizens. The hearings got off to a tumultuous beginning. As statements were read and questioning proceeded, the cause of the El Paso and Juarez valleys was introduced. The sponsor of the bill, Representative Stephens, was emphatic in stating that the proposed international dam would not interfere with existing use in Colorado, but if Elephant Butte were constructed instead, "there will be no flood water for us; there will be no water that will pass El Paso, consequently our dam [the proposed international dam at El Paso] will be worthless, according to their reports. So we are objecting to that dam being built unless they will agree to give us our pro rata share of the water." "The water you have enjoyed before?" he was asked.

"Yes." Stephens then pointed out that it was water "we have enjoyed for three hundred years; that right should be sacred, and the Colorado people should be compelled not to use it and New Mexico should be compelled not to use it."

A friendly discussion followed, in which the watershed and water uses were discussed, all supporting the proposed El Paso dam and detrimental to the Elephant Butte project. Finally L. H. McGowan, a representative of Elephant Butte, could stand it no longer. "You understand, Mr. Chairman, do you not," he interrupted, "that the people representing [the proposed Elephant Butte dam] reverse this whole question and challenge the validity and propriety of the bill. . . ?"

McGowan was then informed that the Elephant Butte attorneys had been asked twice to file a brief but had not done so. McGowan rejoined that the requests had reached them only a few days previously and that they were in process. When asked if he had a statement to make, he said yes and was then given the floor.

He attacked the bill as seeking to "legislate out" the lawsuit pending in the courts, illegally preventing Elephant Butte from using water, and creating a situation that would make it impossible for New Mexicans to water their fields: "Those people represented here and those proposing this international dam, that there might be a distribution of water to Old Mexico and Texas at the expense of New Mexico, induced a suit to be brought against the proposed project."

McGowan then gave a detailed history of New Mexico law concerning the use of water, got into the history of Elephant Butte and its approval by the secretary of the interior, and then treated the question of the flood waters of the Rio Grande. He pointed out that those waters had been utterly wasted, flowing away unused.

They have not contributed even to the little navigation at the mouth 800 miles below, the only navigation there is on the Rio Grande River. After this Elephant Butte scheme was established . . . [a brief resume of its history, repeating what had been said earlier]. They [the opponents of Elephant Butte] declared in their bill [suit] that they brought in the district court of New Mexico, first that we were building a dam or proposing to build a dam, in waters that were navigable, declaring that the waters were navigable at Elephant Butte, and thus making the project obnoxious to the statute of 1890.

McGowan went on to say that when the court found otherwise, the suit (he persisted in calling it a bill) was amended to make it applicable to navigation downstream. The New Mexico court, he reminded everyone, had found that upper Rio Grande waters did not make it to the lower river: "The stream is not navigable in New Mexico at any point, at Elephant Butte, or any place else; that the stream is only navigable from its mouth upward about 250 or 300 miles at most; that the navigation there consists of a single little vessel, the *Bessie,* which only draws 18 inches of water and makes her trips every five or six days when the water is sufficient."

McGowan had the international dam supporters and the government at a disadvantage. If the historical Rio Grande were reconstructed to show its navigability to Laredo, to the Devil's River, in Chihuahua up to and beyond El Paso, or if the single voyage of Howland and Hiester or the ill-fated venture of the Hunt brothers were brought up, there could only be one outcome. Treaties constitute part of the law of the land. They must be enforced. The Treaty of Guadalupe-Hidalgo would have to be enforced, not only on the grounds that the dam would be an obstruction to navigation, but on the grounds of the Seven Parts of law—which New Mexico territorial law violated, as did Colorado's water law system. None of the parties involved—not the United States or Mexican governments or the opponents of Elephant Butte—really wanted that. All they wanted was water for the El Paso and Juarez valleys and to have some control over the Rio Grande as an international boundary.

The New Mexican supporters of Elephant Butte were not even willing to grant that. In the questioning session that followed, McGowan made it perfectly plain that New Mexicans did not consider anyone entitled to waters that the dam would trap—not Old Mexico, not Texas. For, it was pointed out, if the international dam was built at El Paso, there would be no water for New Mexico. While the hearings were going on, engineers of the International Boundary Commission were busy tracing the waters of the upper

Rio Grande all the way to Roma, the presumed head of navigation. They took San Marcial, New Mexico, as the starting point and measured the flow. Then, painstakingly and thoroughly, they followed the waters downstream. At first two calculations were made. One merely measured the amount of flow at San Marcial that was lost to the river at certain points; the other added back waters lost to irrigation below the starting point so that they could obtain a better picture of true evaporation and seepage. The differences were amazing. At El Paso, 38 percent of the San Marcial flow was lost, unless irrigation losses were counted back in; then the flow loss amounted to only 14 percent.[10] Similar results were recorded as far as the Upper Presidio measuring station. Then the dual measurements stopped, although irrigation ditches were measured as far down as Langtry. Perhaps the engineers, taking measurements for the Justice Department, also wanted to measure the losses to the El Paso and Juarez valleys; but if this were the case, they would have stopped dual measurements at Fort Quitman—and certainly would not have measured irrigation down as far as Langtry. No reason for the oversight was ever given in the official report. We can only surmise that as it became increasingly evident that upper Rio Grande waters had, before irrigation below San Marcial, rushed in great volume all the way down to Roma, sticky questions might have been raised as to the effect downstream of the appropriation of waters.

Regardless of the reason, when the long journey to Roma was over, it was discovered that only 16 percent of the San Marcial flow reached Roma, if irrigation losses were not counted. Had the dual measuring system continued, the engineers would have discovered that 55 percent of the San Marcial waters reached Roma. (See Appendix 2.) The engineers presented a picture of the river as it existed in 1900. Sixteen percent of San Marcial flow was about six inches of channel water. Not only did the engineers shy away from the dual measurements, but they also kept from estimating the effect of upper New Mexico and San Luis Valley irrigation on the river. The Justice Department had asked only for a picture of the river as it was, not as it had been or how it would be if no irrigation existed upriver.

While government attorneys prepared their briefs and Boyd's attorneys prepared new ammunition, the entire question of the Rio Grande Dam and

Irrigation Company project was becoming moot. The next time it got to the Supreme Court, the Court would hold that since the five years specified in the charter to build the dam had expired, there was no dam in question.

Down on the lower river, in 1902, an attempt to prove navigability from Laredo was in process. Had Mills or Boyd been aware of it, they would both have had some satisfaction from its results.

John Closner, down at his San Juan Plantation, had need of five huge boilers—each weighing ten thousand pounds—to refine his sugarcane. Since they were too heavy for oxcarts, Closner had to devise a method of bringing them to San Juan Plantation. One boiler was taken off the Texas-Mexican Railway at Peña Station (Hebbronville); from there it was transported to San Juan Plantation—about eighty miles—by rolling it over and over, all the while being pulled by a team of mules. This proved too cumbersome and too costly. The other four boilers were in Laredo awaiting disposition. E. V. Ruthven suggested river transportation, and Closner agreed. A last voyage from Laredo was about to take place.[11]

Ruthven brought two experienced San Jacinto River–Buffalo Bayou pilots down to assist him. A steam barge, sixty feet long with an eighteen-foot beam, was built and equipped with a steam engine and a stern paddlewheel. Each of the boilers was set on deck, the machinery was placed below, and the trip was begun.

All went well until the barge reached the double reef, fifteen miles downriver. The pilots, being unfamiliar with the river, chose to keep to the American shore, rather than make the S-turns required. The barge ground to a halt, hung up on the rocky reef. No amount of coaxing could move her, so the machinery below decks was removed to lighten her draft; but it was not enough. Forty thousand pounds of boiler on deck was too much. Ruthven went downriver a few miles to Nuevo Dolores, where he hired Mercurio Martínez, Sr., and a crew of the town's young men to help get his boat off the reef. They succeeded and took her to Nuevo Dolores. Ruthven did not know what to expect of the river below. It was obvious that his pilots, unfamiliar with the river, could not read it properly. From Laredo, by oxcart, he brought enough lumber to construct four keelboats, one for each boiler. Each boat required four oarsmen and a helmsman, who were hired at the town, Martínez being put in charge. The empty big barge and four smaller keelboats went on downstream, with but one minor incident at the island just above the Salado. There the barge grounded but was pulled free with little trouble. The rest of the trip was made without problems. Whatever became of the barge and her little sisters is unrecorded.

One wonders why Closner did not have the boilers shipped to Point Isabel, taken by rail to Brownsville, and then brought up to the plantation by the *Bessie*. Even if each boiler required a separate trip from Brownsville, it would have been quicker, cheaper, and surer. Was Closner thinking about the possibility of using the railhead at Laredo for profitable trade, or was the entire adventure a mistaken play, meant to prove nothing?

General Anson Mills, had he been aware of the navigation attempt, would probably have pointed to it as proof that the river was navigable up to Laredo; Dr. Nathan Boyd might have agreed that it was navigable to the Salado, but no farther. At any rate, Boyd would have added that no water from New Mexico or Colorado ever got there, no matter what Commissioner Mills's engineers said.

Although a private dam at Elephant Butte was a dead issue, emotions were running high in the Juarez and El Paso valleys and New Mexico. The international dam at El Paso was now the only choice offered, since Elephant Butte had been declared moot. Many felt that it would be better to have no dam at all; others proposed a government dam at Elephant Butte—one to guarantee water only to New Mexico farmers. Mexico began to press her claims with renewed vigor, as did Texas farmers. The New Mexicans wanted water as well. Each group feared that no matter what transpired, two claimants would be left without the means to irrigate.

Then, in 1904, an irrigation congress was convened in El Paso. Delegates from Mexico, Texas, the United States, and New Mexico attended. The results were historic. G. A. Martin, writing in an El Paso newspaper in 1923, best described the background and the congress.

Eighteen and a half years ago, New Mexico, Texas, the United States, and Mexico effected an agreement that made possible the great Elephant Butte Reclamation Project. Prior to that time, Mexico was pressing a claim for many millions of dollars against the United States for using all the waters in the Rio Grande before it reached this point [El Paso and the entrance to the Mother Ditch]. New Mexico was insisting on building a dam at Elephant Butte to water the lands north of here, and El Paso was insisting on a dam near the smelter to water the lands below El Paso in Texas. All claimants had a just and equitable right to the water. Mexico, possibly, had first right, as it was irrigating lands below Juarez and El Paso for agricultural land and horticultural purposes when the first Europeans visited this section. New Mexico had also used water at a very early period. Colorado irrigationists had impounded and used much of the water. . . . New Mexico was getting none. . . , and El Paso Valley farmers but little.[12]

When the irrigation congress met, the delegates did nothing but argue the same claims; none was willing to admit the others' right to water, fearing that he would lose his. Then, in the midst of debate and turmoil, Major R. F. Burges offered a resolution to the effect that a dam be built at Elephant Butte and the waters be divided equitably. His resolution provided a water supply for all, and it was accepted. Martin tells it this way:

As one man, the five Mexican delegates arose and bowed, giving their consent in this manner. The late L. Bradford Prince, former Governor of New Mexico, was presiding. He said he believed this was a happy solution to the matter, put it to a vote, and the convention adopted it unanimously.

A formal document was drawn up and later signed. In essence, the congress voted to have the United States government build the dam and divide and distribute the waters impounded. A treaty was drawn up in 1906 and ratified in 1907 between the United States and Mexico. The United States would do just that at its own expense, guaranteeing Mexico 60,000 acre feet of water annually, delivered to the Mother Ditch. In return, Mexico would drop all claims against the United States.

Burges's motion was made on the spur of the moment. He was not even a delegate; he and a friend, Julius Frakauer, were sitting together, watching the fruitless debate. The two had been discussing possible solutions to the problem when Burges got the idea. "Put it to a motion," Frakauer said. "They won't know if you're a delegate or not."

Thus are great debates resolved. Elephant Butte would be built, not by the Rio Grande Dam and Irrigation Company but by the United States government. What trickles of water still reached the lower river would be cut off. From the time of Elephant Butte, the Rio Grande from the Gulf to Presidio del Norte would be supplied by the Conchos. None of her upper waters would ever again freshen the arid lands below Fort Quitman or float river steamers. Down at Brownsville, the *Bessie* had made her last trip, a shallowing river, more than railroads, finally bringing her long career to an end. The average western riverboat lasted about five years in active service;[13] the *Bessie* had served the lower Rio Grande for twenty-eight years before being tied up and retired. She disintegrated at dockside in 1907.

But navigation was not over. In 1910 a hurricane devastated the lower river. Torrential rains produced massive flooding; banks washed away, the riverbed shifted a little, and the boundary markers were lost. Commissioner Mills sent W. W. Follett to the lower river to remark the boundary and reset the markers.

Follett was familiar with the lower river, having made several surveys of it. He had been along with Mills in 1894 when a flatboat had been used to mark boundaries and take damage claim testimony, so he was not a novice. But he had not been on the lower river since 1900/01, when he took part in the measurement of waters from the upper Rio Grande. Those few years had made a difference. He designed a thirty-five-foot launch—the *Leslie.* She was powered by a twenty-five-horsepower gasoline engine and drew thirty inches of water. Follett used her to pull two houseboats, one that was ten feet by thirty feet and used for an office and sleeping, and another ten feet by twenty feet, used for cooking and dining. In addition, the work party had a twenty-foot dory with a five-horsepower engine, a fourteen-foot skiff with a small gasoline engine, and four twelve-foot rowing skiffs. It was quite a flotilla that he put on the river. Follett was a good hydroengineer; he was not a river-marine engineer. His launch drew too much water, should have had a paddlewheel instead of a propeller, and should have had a bottom designed for towing. Follett found these things out for himself.

In his report he wrote, "During the whole season the river was low, and

The gasoline launch *Leslie* passing houseboats during the remarking of the boundary following the hurricane of 1910. From *Supplemental Report of the American Engineer.* Courtesy Russell Brown.

much difficulty was experienced in navigating it with the launch. . . . One mile above the San Juan there was an impassable rapids, so the boats were left there and the work near Roma was done from a land camp."[14]

The river had changed a great deal in nine years. Follett noted that his launch drew nearly three and a half feet of water when towing the houseboats, and he complained that it frequently got hung up on bars while the two houseboats floated on. The propeller shaft was finally twisted on one of these bars. A paddlewheel would have cleared them or walked over them, and a proper bottom design would have allowed the tow to progress in an even fashion. After the survey was completed, Follett left the *Leslie* with the Corps of Engineers in Galveston. It was the last attempt to navigate the changed Rio Grande successfully.

For a century and a half the river had drawn men to her, creating dreams of power and prestige and wealth; the fulfillment of those dreams lay in navigation. The natural phenomenon of the Rio Grande caught up the ambitious, the scheming, the altruistic. She should have been opened

This marker describing the *Bessie*'s bell illustrates the way folklore and history become intertwined. Kenedy and King never owned the boat, which steamed on the Rio Grande from 1876 to 1904. Courtesy Burt Johnson.

to the Devil's River—even the pragmatic Major William Emory had predicted that.[15] She had room for all, and she succumbed only to the ever-
lasting needs of a desert, the economics of climate and settlement overwhelming those who dreamed of creating what could never be. When
events beyond one's control crush a dream, one must recoup and find
other ways to glory. The Great River did just that. Elephant Butte ended one
era, but it began another.

Appendix 1

Merchant and Government Vessels on the Rio Grande

The following list is as complete as I could make it. Some United States Quartermaster vessels may have been omitted, but primarily because no record could be found of their entering the Rio Grande above Boca del Rio. Readers who know of vessels not included are asked to let the writer know about them.

Abbreviations	sd, sidewheeler	g, gasoline engine	*, information not
	st, sternwheeler	k, keel boat	yet found
	p, propeller	f, flatboat	U, unknown

Name of vessel	Rig	Tons	Year	Place built	Rio Grande owners
Aid	sd	137	1843	Cincinnati	Charles Stillman

(Advertised in *American Flag* in 1849 as being owned by E. W. Gemmill)

Name of vessel	Rig	Tons	Year	Place built	Rio Grande owners
Alamo	st	120	1861	Wheeling, Virginia	Edward Downey
Alamosa	p	*	1874	Alamosa, Colorado	Bert and Bruce Hunt
Alice	*	*	*	*	*
Anson	sd	U	U	U	USQMD
Antonia	sd	*	1865	Brownsville, Texas	Kenedy & Co. Government of France King, Kenedy & Co.
Ariel	sd	86	1825	New York, N.Y.	Henry Austin

(*Ariel* was the first U.S.-owned steamboat on the Rio Grande [1829] and the first steamboat on the Brazos River, Texas [1830]. She foundered on the bar of the Brazos River and limped her way to Buffalo Bayou. Abandoned in the San Jacinto River on December 29, 1830.)

Name of vessel	Rig	Tons	Year	Place built	Rio Grande owners
Bessie	st	100	1876	St. Louis	O. B. Filley William Kelly
Big Hatchee	st	195	1844	Pittsburgh	USQMD
Brownsville	sd	99	1845	Louisville	USQMD Bodman & Clark
Camargo	st	*	*	*	M. Kenedy & Co.

(Sunk at her moorings at White Ranch, Texas, by the hurricane of October 1867.)

Camargo II	sd	92	1865	Algiers, Louisiana	King, Kenedy & Co.

(Although the dates do not seem to coincide, it is probable that the *Camargo II* was a Mexican-registered Civil War boat brought back into service after the hurricane of October 1867.)

Casimir Castro	P	U	U	U	U
Colonel Cross	sd	160	1846	Shousetown, Pennsylvania	USQMD Robert Penny & Richard King
Colonel Harney	sd	132	1844	Port Fulton, Indiana	USQMD
Colonel Holcomb	sd	373	1864	Algiers, Louisiana	U.S. Government Mifflin Kenedy & R. King John Stone
Colonel Hunt	sd	214	1847	Louisville	USQMD
Colonel John Stevens	p	155	1845	Philadelphia	USQMD
Colonel Stanton	st	138	1847	Philadelphia	USQMD
Comanche	st	164	1850	Freedom, Pennsylvania	M. Kenedy & Co.
Cora	sd	179	1845	New Albany, Indiana	U
Corvette	sd	149	1846	Brownsville, Pennsylvania	USQMD
Del Norte	st	114	1846	Zanesville, Ohio	Bodman & Clark M. Kenedy & Co.

Name of vessel	Rig	Tons	Year	Place built	Rio Grande owners
De Rosset	sd	186	1839	Baltimore	USQMD
Don Juan Closner	st	*	1902	Laredo, Texas	John Closner
Dragon	sd	U	U	U	USQMD
El Primero	st	90	1865	Brownsville, Texas	W. R. Verlander Kenedy & Co. King, Kenedy & Co.
Enterprise	sd	106	1844	Cincinnati	Chartered by USQMD
Enterprise	sd	U	1865	Brownsville, Texas	W. R. Verlander Kenedy & Co.

(Sunk at her moorings at White Ranch, Texas, by the hurricane of October 1867.)

Name of vessel	Rig	Tons	Year	Place built	Rio Grande owners
Eugenia	sd	134	1865	Newburgh, N.Y.	Benito Vinas Government of France Benito Vinas Sold Foreign
Exchange	sd	75	1845	New Albany, Indiana	USQMD

(In 1853 Major Emory mentioned seeing the ruins of an *Exchange* above present day Zapata.)

Name of vessel	Rig	Tons	Year	Place built	Rio Grande owners
Exchange	sd	U	U	U	U

(This vessel, advertised in 1849 as being on a schedule between Brownsville and Roma, foundered near Roma and was raised and refitted. She may be the vessel listed above.)

Name of vessel	Rig	Tons	Year	Place built	Rio Grande owners
Fashion	sd	419	1842	New York, N.Y.	USQMD
Frankland	sd	96	1845	Knoxville	Charles Stillman Bodman & Clark
Frontier	sd	109	1843	Louisville	U
Gazelle	sd	92	1844	Cincinnati	Robert Penny
General Hamel	U	U	U	U	U

(The only *General Hamel* in the Lytle-Holdcamper list was built in 1849; this vessel was in use on the Rio Grande in 1847.)

Name of vessel	Rig	Tons	Year	Place built	Rio Grande owners
General Jessup	sd	374	1847	Elizabethtown, Pennsylvania	USQMD
Globe	p	461	1842	New York, N.Y.	U

(Plied a scheduled route between Brazos Santiago and Galveston. In high water she would go to Brownsville.)

Name of vessel	Rig	Tons	Year	Place built	Rio Grande owners
Grampus	sd	221	1850	Freedom, Pennsylvania	M. Kenedy & R. King
Grampus No. 2	sd	252	1856	McKeesport, Pennsylvania	M. Kenedy & R. King
Guadalupe	sd	137	1852	West Elizabeth, Pennsylvania	J. B. Armstrong Richard King, M. Kenedy, & Charles Stillman
Harry Love	k		1849	Brazos Santiago	USQMD
Hatchee Eagle	sd	116	1845	Louisville	USQMD Samuel A. Belden
J. E. Roberts	sd	118	1844	Grave Neck, Virginia	USQMD Bodman & Clark
J. S. Sellers (*A. S. Sellers?*)	sd	186	1869	Galveston	Robert Dabzell Mifflin Kenedy Richard King Joseph Cooper Jeremiah Galvan
				Last Document 1872	Francisco Yturria
James Hale	st	173	1850	Freedom, Pennsylvania	M. Kenedy & Co.
Jerry Galvan	st	98	1865	Brownsville, Texas	M. Kenedy & Richard King
Jessie B.	*	*	*	*	U
John Scott	*	*	*	*	U
Josephine	sd	*	*	*	USQMD

(A small 26-barrel capacity boat used between Brazos Santiago and Point Isabel 1849–50. She made occasional trips to Fort Brown when necessary.)

Name of vessel	Rig	Tons	Year	Place built	Rio Grande owners
Jose San Roman	sd	400	1865	Pittsburgh	Robert Dabzell
					Joseph Cooper
					Mifflin Kenedy
					King, Kenedy & Co.
					Jeremiah Galvan
					Francisco Yturria
				Last listed in 1872	A. H. Brown
Lama	sd	68	1844	Cincinnati	U
Laura	sd	26	1845	Pittsburgh	U
Laurel	sd	*	*	*	Bodman & Clark
Leo	sd	82	1842	*	Sam M. Williams
Leslie	pg	Launch		Camden, N.J.	Int. Boundary Commission
Louisa	st	27	1864	Algiers, Louisiana	U.S. Government J. W. Warren
Lulu D.	*	*	*	*	King, Kenedy & Co.
Luzon	p	*	*	*	*
Major Babbitt	k	U	1850	Brazos Santiago	USQMD
Major Brown	st	125	1846	Elizabeth, Pennsylvania	USQMD
Major Tompkins	p	141	1847	Philadelphia	USQMD
Mamie	sd	45	1865	Clarksville, Texas	W. R. Verlander
Manteo	p	*	*	*	*
Maria Burt	sd	319	1846	Cincinnati	USQMD
Matamoros	sd	278	1860	Shousetown, Pennsylvania	U.S. Government Robert Dabzell M. Kenedy & R. King

Name of vessel	Rig	Tons	Year	Place built	Rio Grande owners
					Document surrendered 1869, "worn out"
Matamoros No. 2	sd	241	1869	Pittsburgh	Robert Dabzell Mifflin Kenedy Richard King Joseph Cooper Jeremiah Galvan Francisco Yturria A. H. Brown
McGuffin	f	4	1874	Santa Fe	Howland & Hiester
Mentoria	sd	106	1845	Cincinnati	USQMD M. Kenedy & Co.
Mexico	*	U	U	U	U
Monmouth	p	*	1836	Baltimore	USQMD
Monroe	sd	126	1845	Monroe, Alabama	Hugh Monroe
Mustang	*	*	*	*	U
Neva	sd	144	1841	Louisville	USQMD
Ranchero	st	206	1854	Freedom, Pennsylvania	Richard King, M. Kenedy, & Charles Stillman
Rough and Ready	sd	150	1846	Elizabethtown, Pennsylvania	USQMD
S. J. Lee	st	176	1866	Galveston	A. J. Moose Perry Doddridge Richard King H. Mathis C. A. Hartshorn Perry Doddridge Manuel de Siane Sold to Galveston owner, then to Rio Grande Railroad Company M. de Lano

Name of vessel	Rig	Tons	Year	Place built	Rio Grande owners
Sabine	sd	106	1843	Louisville	U
San Juan	st	214	1871	Pittsburgh	Robert Dabzell Mifflin Kenedy Richard King Joseph Cooper Francisco Yturria Jeremiah Galvan A. H. Brown
Santiago	sd	96	1865	Brownsville, Texas	M. Kenedy & R. King
Senorita	*	*	*	*	Kenedy & Co.

(Was chartered by the French for use as a gunboat during their intervention. Reacquired by King, Kenedy & Co. in 1866.)

Swan	st	127	1851	Jeffersonville, Indiana	J. B. Armstrong R. King, M. Kenedy, & Charles Stillman
Tamaulipas No. 1	st	206	1863	Wilmington, Delaware	USQMD Fred W. Noble Mifflin Kenedy Half interest to Richard King
Tamaulipas No. 2	st	201	1864	Pittsburgh	Richard King M. Kenedy & Co. Jos. Cooper Robert Dabzell Jeremiah Galvan Francisco Yturria Last listed owner, 1868, A. H. Brown
Tangipahoa	sd	60	1832	Cincinnati	George Wilbor

(In all likelihood, the first vessel to reach Laredo, 1834.)

Telegraph	sd	330	1836	Philadelphia	USQMD
Tom Kirkman	sd	120	1846	Louisville	U Charles Stillman Listed as "For

Name of vessel	Rig	Tons	Year	Place built	Rio Grande owners
					Sale" in 1849 by her owner, Peter Dowd
Tom McKinney	sd	168	1848	Galveston	Williams & P. H. Collier Advertised in 1849 as being operated by her master, Capt. Miller
Troy	st	92	1846	Louisville	U.S. Government Samuel A. Belden
Undine	*	197	1845	Cincinnati	USQMD
Undine	sd	*	*	*	U

U (the Bradburn and Staples vessel of 1828)

U (the vessel of 1834)	U
U (the vessel of 1837)	U

U (at least 6 keelboats owned by Alpheus Rackliffe)

U (A Camargo ferry used as a flatboat for an inspection of changes in the course of the Rio Grande by the International Boundary and Water Commission in 1894. Before the survey was completed, Camargo wanted the boat back, so the commissioners placed it on a passing steamboat, the *Bessie,* and shipped it back.)

Name of vessel	Rig	Tons	Year	Place built	Rio Grande owners
Virginia	sd	296	1845	New York, N.Y.	U
Warren	sd	109	1846	Aurora, Indiana	USQMD
Whiteville (or *Whitesville*)	sd	102	1844	Pittsburgh	USQMD Samuel A. Belden
William Newton Mercer	*	113	1845	Savannah, Tennessee	USQMD
William R. McKee	sd	165	1845	Cincinnati	USQMD
Yazoo	sd	44	1849	Point Isabel, Texas	USQMD U

Appendix 2

Flow of the Rio Grande as It Affected Navigation

If we are to comprehend the meaning of irrigation to navigation on the Rio Grande fully, we must make a complete study of the effects of irrigation beginning in 1850. In order to do so, we must correlate the International Boundary (Water) Commission survey of 1900/01 and the commission's irrigation study of 1896. In the former, the commission engineers took San Marcial as their starting point for measuring losses of upriver water flowing to Roma. At selected points they measured flow loss. They calculated the percentage of flow reaching these points first, not taking irrigation diversions into consideration, and second, adding back irrigation losses in order to get a true picture of loss due to seepage and evaporation only. A comparison of the two methods of computation, taken from commission tables, shows the effect of irrigation below San Marcial.[1] One can understand the necessity of filling in the blanks if an accurate picture of the navigable Rio Grande is to be painted.

Table 1: Comparing San Marcial flow by (1) not taking irrigation below San Marcial into account, and (2) taking that irrigation into account. Percentages show the amount of San Marcial flow lost.

Station	Method 1	Method 2	% Difference
El Paso	38	14	271
Fort Hancock	53	21	252
Upper Presidio	74	35*	211
Devil's River	80	—	—
Eagle Pass	81	—	—
Roma	84	—	—

*Given as 39 percent in commission tables; however, in the text of the journal, they arrived at the figure given here.[2]

Since the commission included measurements of all irrigation ditches as far as Langtry (above San Felipe Springs) but did not use those below the Upper Presidio measuring station, that flow, considering losses by irrigation, would have to be evaluated to show the true loss caused by seepage and evaporation. Fortunately, the commission engineers included a table showing rates of flow at pertinent recording stations of the San Marcial waters, taking into account increases caused by tributaries, springs, and local rainfall.[3] It was from these readings that the raw percentage (not taking into account diversions for irrigation) for each was calculated. In order to reflect only evaporation and seepage, the commission added in waters lost to irrigation before each station as far as the Upper Presidio. To fill in the blanks in Table 1, then, waters lost to irrigation must be taken into account for Devil's River, Eagle Pass, and Roma. The constant figure for irrigation diversion is 1,496 cubic feet per second, the amount measured between the Upper Presidio station and Langtry, near the Devil's River station.[4] Adjusting for irrigation losses, then, we arrive at a very conservative estimate of flow from San Marcial, allowing for evaporation and seepage, that reached each point.

Using the methods employed by the commission, percentage of loss allowing for irrigation diversions, the missing information in Table 1 is filled in.

Table 2

Station	Method 1 No Diversions	Method 2 With Diversions	% Difference
Devil's River	80	40.45	198
Eagle Pass	81	41	197.6
Roma	84	45	186.67

To put the table into positives, the amount of water reaching each point from San Marcial results in the following:

Table 3: Percentage of water reaching each station, each method considered

Station	Method 1	Method 2
Devil's River	20.0	59.55
Eagle Pass	19.0	59.0
Roma	16.0	55.0

One should keep in mind that, in later tables, the percentages above are treated as constants—that is, 55 percent of whatever the San Marcial flow happened to be should have reached Roma if no irrigation took place.

IRRIGATION LOSSES ABOVE SAN MARCIAL

The commission survey failed to take into consideration irrigation losses above San Marcial. To get an accurate picture of the effects of those losses on the lower river, they must be taken into consideration. The next two tables illustrate the growth of irrigation following 1850 in the upper reaches.

There is a probable error of 10 percent when considering irrigation, because of the quality of records kept prior to 1880.[5] After 1880 there is virtually no error in irrigation figures. Because irrigation took place exclusively in the period April through September, all irrigation is considered to have taken place during the high water period of the river.

Table 4:[6] Growth of irrigation in the San Luis
Valley, 1850–79, first-time use only (in acre feet)

District	1850–59	1860–69	1870–79	Cumulative
20			27,000	27,000
21		1,840	18,015	19,855
22	41,830	6,540	9,035	57,405
24	25,480	1,560	405	27,445
25		2,254	115,051	117,305
26		1,980	5,538	7,518
27			16,349	16,349
35			5,990	5,990
Totals	67,310	14,174	197,383	278,867

These figures represent first-time use only. By 1896 annual use of Rio Grande water in the San Luis Valley totaled, depending on rainfall, between 559,290 acre feet (the least used) and 950,570 acre feet (a more typical figure).

Table 5:[7] Irrigation in New Mexico, 1850–79, first-time use only (in acre feet)

District	Pre-1850	1850–59	1860–69	1870–79	1850–79
1				5,080	5,080
2	23,130	24,450	23,880	12,330	60,660
3	3,780	8,440		2,600	11,040
4	13,520	9,250	2,160		11,410
5	19,790			560	560
6	12,750				
7	10,509				
8	4,350				
9	14,550				
10	18,076	2,600	3,300	1,030	6,930
11	800		1,860	1,180	3,040
12	44,280				
13	32,280				
14	57,070		750		750
15	12,570	2,370	2,000		4,370
16			3,050	3,200	6,250
17	25,250	28,500	7,250	1,500	37,250
Totals	252,856	75,610	44,250	27,480	147,340

As in the San Luis Valley, the upper New Mexico figures for 1850–79 represent first year use only. By 1896, up to 551,390 acre feet were being taken from the river each summer.

RIVER FLOW ABOVE SAN MARCIAL

River flows cannot be as accurately estimated, since no gauges were in use until late in the period under consideration and flow figures above Embudo may have a 30 percent error.[8] In order to arrive at a usable figure, available flows were averaged, and it was assumed that the average would give a reasonable estimate of prior years. The estimates are, if anything, too low, since as settlement grew, timber was stripped from the lower elevations. The denuding of timber allowed winter snows to melt prematurely, and their waters went into winter flow, being lost to the summer season. Prior to heavy settlement, the snows remained packed until the spring thaw.

Table 6:[9] River Flows Omitting and Including Irrigation Losses (in acre feet)

Seven-year (1890–96) average summer flow at Del Norte *516,332.85 (headwater point of measurement)*

Seven year (1890–96) average summer flow at Embudo *666,497.* Taking into consideration water lost to irrigation, the flow *should have been 1,305,927 acre feet.*

Four-year (1890–93) average summer flow at San Marcial *1,074,570.* Allowing for up-river irrigation, increase of flow due to tributaries, and losses due to seepage and evaporation, the figure reads *2,349,031 acre feet.* Pre-1850 irrigation is excluded.

The following table illustrates the effect of first time irrigation, cumulative, upon the river.

Table 7: Estimated flow of Rio Grande at San Marcial[10] and at selected points (in acre feet)

Station	*Pre-1850*	*1850–59*	*1860–69*	*1870–79*	*1880–1901*
San Marcial	2,263,423	2,206,111	2,147,687	1,922,824	538,408
San Marcial flow passing:					
Devil's River	1,437,868				113,066
Eagle Pass	1,335,418				107,682
Roma	1,233,883	1,042,593	851,305	660,013	86,145

(All flows, pre-1850, are based on Table 3. Those for 1880–1901 are based on Table 1.)

Taking the results of the ten-day measurements (see Table 2) as indicative of summer flow, it is possible to set up a ratio of San Marcial flow to Roma flow that will indicate loss of channel depth at Roma. Sixteen percent of San Marcial flow equaled .5 feet of channel depth when that flow was measured at Roma. Comparisons between the Rio Grande before 1850 with each decade following produce the following table.

Table 8: Loss of channel depth at Roma, Pre-1850 to 1901

	Pre-1850	1850–59	1860–69	1870–79	1880–1901
Loss in feet	0	1.11	2.58	3.83	7.16

When Elephant Butte Dam was completed, all flow of upper waters was cut off. The channel depth at Roma dropped another 6 inches, making a total channel loss of 7.66 feet.

Notes

CHAPTER 1

1 The lower river is so described by its early viewers, among them Tienda de Cuervo, Santa María, and Calleja.

2 This description of the channel to the entrance of the Conchos River (near present-day Presidio, Texas) is based on written reports of actual navigators and of some who collected such reports. All are cited in Chapters 2 through 4. The possibility of navigation from Eagle's Tail Mountain to above El Paso is based on official reports of the state of Chihuahua. Distances given are by the river and are rounded off from figures furnished by the International Boundary and Water Commission office in Laredo.

3 Television documentary, James Irby and Pat Kelley, *Search por el conquistador* (Edinburg: Pan American University Learning Resource Center, 1978).

4 Mexican historians, and some American ones, claim that Pineda entered the Panuco River, not the Rio Grande. A careful perusal of documents and maps relating to this voyage tends to negate this theory. For example, from the Rio de las Palmas, the expedition traveled south to the Panuco.

5 Hubert J. Miller, *José de Escandón: Colonizer of Nuevo Santander* (Edinburg: New Santander Press, 1980), pp. 6–24.

6 *Estados general de las fundaciones hechas por don José de Escandón en la colonia del Nuevo Santander* (Mexico City: Talleres Gráficos de la Nación, 1930), 2: 9–11.

7 Information on Laredo contained in the de Cuervo report is taken from Herbert Eugene Bolton, trans. and ed., "Tienda de Cuervo's *Inspección* of Laredo," *Texas Historical Association Quarterly* (January 1903): 187–203. Information on Reynosa, Camargo, Revilla, and Hacienda de Dolores is from *Estados general*, 1: 31–37.

8 Jerry Thompson, *Sabers on the Rio Grande* (Austin: Presidial Press, 1974), p. 15.

9 *Inventory of County Archives of Texas, No. 240, Webb County (Laredo) (Historical Records Survey)* (February 1938): 14.

10 Henry R. Wagner, *The Spanish Southwest, 1542–1794* (New York: Arno Press, 1967), 1: 481–82.

11 Alejandro Prieto, *Historia, geográfica, y estadística de Tamaulipas* (Mexico City: Manuel Porrus, Librio, 1949), pp. 481–83. A reissue of the 1873 edition.

12 Helen B. Foster, "Steamship Navigation in Pennsylvania" (M.A. thesis, Pennsylvania State College, 1933), pp. 3, 4.

13 Fr. Vicente Santa María, *Relación histórica de la colonia del Nuevo Santander y costa del seno mexicano,* in *Estado general,* 2: 371, 372.

14 Although *Inventory* lists local produce in all the river towns as the basis of a flatboat trade, it is far more likely that contraband tobacco was the medium of exchange. All the river settlements produced very nearly the same products except for the salt of Reynosa. Spanish inspectors and officials complained chronically of the loss of revenues from contraband tobacco. See a letter from Mariscal al Virrey, June 12, 1767, written from Laredo, in the microfilm collection of the Tamaulipas Archives in Victoria concerning the inspection of 1767/68 (no. 13, f. 323).

15 Santa María, *Relación histórica,* p. 382.

16 Thompson, *Sabers,* p. 16.

17 *Inventory,* p. 41.

18 Felix Calleja del Rey, "Nuevo Santander in 1795: A Provincial Inspection," trans. and ed. David M. Vigness, *Southwestern Historical Quarterly* (April 1972): 461–596. All biographical information on Calleja is taken from this source and from Manuel García Purón, *México y sus gobernantes* (Mexico City: Libreria de Manuel Porrúa, 1964), pp. 148, 149. All direct quotes are from Vigness.

19 Biographical information on John Davis Bradburn is based on information found in Margaret Swett Henson, *Juan Davis Bradburn* (College Station: Texas A&M University Press, 1982), pp. 40–155.

20 Teodoro Ortiz y Ayala, *Resumen de la estadística del imperio mexicano,* ed. Tarsicio García Díaz (Mexico City: Universidad Nacional Autónoma de México, 1968), pp. 10–11.

21 Biographical material on Ortiz y Ayala is taken from Wilbert H. Timmons, *Teodoro Ortiz de Ayala: Mexican Colonizer and Reformer* (El Paso: Texas Western Press, 1974), pp. 5–16.

22 Ortiz y Ayala, *Resumen de la estadística,* p. 85. The particular work referred to, *Ideario mexicano,* is included as Appendix 1; each page is summarized rather than reprinted verbatim. This quote is from page 110 of the original, which corresponds to paragraph 110 in Appendix 1.

23 Manuel Dublan y José María Lozano, *Disposiciones legislativas desde la independencia de la república, Edición oficial* (Mexico City: Imprenta del Comercio, a Cargo de Dublan y Lozano, Hijos, 1876), 1: 738, 739.

CHAPTER 2

1 Manuel García Purón, *México y sus gobernantes* (Mexico City: Libreria de Manuel Porrúa, 1964). An actual count of those who claimed the presidency of Mexico between 1821 and 1831.

2 Information on the de León–LaFon venture can be found in Tom Lea, *The King Ranch* (Toronto: Little, Brown & Co., 1957), pp. 47, 48, and in A. B. J. Hammett, *The Empresario Don Martín de León* (Kerrville, Tex.: Braswell Printing Company, 1971), p. 13. Information on Matamoros is from José Raúl Conseco, *Historia de Matamoros,* n.d. The book is offset from a typescript. The section cited is titled "Antecedentes históricos," which covers Matamoros to the year 1824; Lea, *The King Ranch,* pp. 1–176, passim; Jean Louis Berlandier, *Journey to Mexico During the Years 1826 to 1834,* trans. and ed. Sheila M. Ohlendorf, Josette M. Bigelow, and Mary M. Standifer (Austin: Texas State Historical Association, 1980), 2 vols. References to the history of Matamoros are scattered throughout both volumes. The work actually covers the years to 1838 or 1839. Berlandier never finished it and went beyond his title when writing it.

3 Information on Stephen McL. Staples is gleaned from the microfilm collection made available by the British Foreign and Commonwealth Office, Public Records Office. The collection covering the years 1811–40 in Mexico is held by Laredo State University. Some information on Staples is in J. J. Bowden, "The Texas–New Mexico Boundary Dispute," *Southwestern Historical Quarterly* (October 1959): 222–23.

4 Berlandier, *Journey to Mexico,* 1: 267, 268.

5 The article cited from *Espíritu público* is taken from a clipping sent to London by the British consul and is part of the microfilm collection mentioned in note 4.

No date is ascribed to the clipping, but it must have preceded March 18, when Chihuahua granted the concession to Bradburn and Staples.

6 Decree of March 18, 1828, by the governor of Chihuahua.

7 *The Laws of Texas, 1822–1897,* ed. H. P. N. Gammel (Austin: Gammel Book Company, 1898), 1: 210, 211.

8 Berlandier, *Journey to Mexico,* 1: 268.

9 William H. Egerton, *Important Report Just Received from the Government Surveyor for the Tracts of Land owned by The Rio Grande and Texas Land Co.* (New York: Osborn and Buckingham, Printers, 1835), p. 6.

10 Margaret Swett Henson, *Juan Davis Bradburn* (College Station: Texas A&M University Press, 1982), pp. 44–46.

11 Secretario de Despacho del Estado de Chihuahua, *Memoria sobre la administración pública del estado, Leyda al honorable congreso, Tercero constitucional, en 4 de julio, 1831* (Mexico City: C. José Sabino Cano, 1831), p. 26.

12 Henry Austin's misadventures in Mexico have been covered many times. Sources used include *Annual Report of the American Historical Association for the Year 1922: The Austin Papers,* vol. 2; Paul Horgan, *Great River: The Rio Grande in North American History* (New York: Holt, Rinehart and Winston, 1971), pp. 481–94 and scattered references; and William Ransom Hogan, "Henry Austin," *Southwestern Historical Quarterly* (January 1934): 185–214.

13 Berlandier, *Journey to Mexico,* 1: 441; Bryant P. Tilden, *Notes on the Upper Rio Grande* (Philadelphia: Lindsay and Blakiston, 1847). The reference to the draft of the *Ariel* is on a chart of the river.

14 Sources for Alpheus Rackliffe's involvement with the Rio Grande include Tilden, *Notes,* dedication; and references to flatboat trade or flatboats on the river in Thomas Jefferson Green, *Journal of the Texian Expedition against Mier, Subsequent Imprisonment of the Author, His Sufferings and Final Escape from the Castle Perote, with Reflections upon the Present Political and Probable Future Relations of Texas, Mexico, and the United States* (Austin: Steck Company, 1935; reprint of 1844 ed.), pp. 67–74; and in Egerton, *Important Report,* p. 6. Most helpful, however, were the efforts of his descendants living in Laredo, Lily Perez and Helen Peña, who managed to locate one of his journals. It was mostly filled with praise for the beautiful young lady he had seen but also contained much information.

15 *American Flag,* a Matamoros-Brownsville newspaper of the Mexican War period,

indicates in almost every extant issue that the river was more difficult than the western rivers because of its swift current and twistings.

16 Egerton, *Important Report*, p. 6.

17 Leroy P. Graf, "Economic History of the Lower Rio Grande Valley, 1820–1875" (Ph.D. diss., Harvard University, 1940), section on navigation, cites American consul at Matamoros as source for the *Tanqipahoa*. He also lists other vessels mentioned, as does Berlandier, *Journey to Mexico*, 1: 268.

18 In a letter quoted by Charles Edwards, *Texas and Coahuila, with an Exposition of the Last Colonization Law, (28th day of April, 1932)* (New York: S. Decamp & Co., 1834), p. 19.

19 Information on Beales's life and the Rio Grande and Texas Land Company is taken from John Henry Brown, *History of Texas from 1685 to 1892* (Austin: Jenkins Publishing Company, 1970; reprint of 1892 ed.), 1: 254–56; and from William Kennedy, *The Rise, Progress, and Prospects of the Republic of Texas, 2nd. Edition, London* (Fort Worth: Molyneaux Craftsmen, Inc., 1923; reprint of 1841 ed.), pp. 390, 391.

20 Charles Edwards, *Rio Grande and Texas Land Company* (New York: n.p., 1834).

21 Beales's diary is cited verbatim in Kennedy, *Republic of Texas*, pp. 392–419. Ludecus's day-by-day account, which parallels Beales's, is in the form of letters and comes from Eduard Ludecus, *Reise durch die mexikanischen Provinzen Tamaulipas, Coahuila und Texas, im Jahre 1834*, chapters 10–16, trans. B. Brandt (Leipzig: n.p., 1837), typescript. The copy I used was courtesy of Mrs. Salle Stemmons of Dallas, who is the great-great-granddaughter of Ludecus. The typescript is limited to that portion of the book that deals with the colony of Dolores.

22 Egerton, *Important Report*, pp. 1, 2.

23 Berlandier, *Journey to Mexico*, 1: 268, 2: 442–43.

24 J. A. de Escudero, *Noticias estadísticas del estado de Chihuahua* (Mexico City: En la Oficina del Puente de Palacio y Flamencos num. 1, por Juan Ojeda, 1834), pp. 195–97.

25 Edwards, *Rio Grande and Texas*, p. 7.

26 *Matagorda Bulletin*, July 5, 1838.

27 Green, *Journal of the Texian Expedition*, pp. 68–73.

28 "Letter, Charles Elliot to Lord Aberdeen, December 2d, 1843," *Southwestern Historical Quarterly* 18:1 (July 1914): 83.

CHAPTER 3

1 Brevet Major W. W. Chapman, assistant quartermaster for the District of the Rio Grande, mentions in many letters the ways and their uses. See particularly letters to Jessup, October 28, 1848, and Thomas, October 31, 1848. Quartermaster General Consolidated Files, Group 92, Navy and Old Army Archives, National Archives, Washington, D.C. Cited hereafter as Quartermaster General Files.

2 This was a favorite saying of Rio Grande boatmen.

3 Brevet Major W. W. Chapman to General Thomas S. Jessup, September 5, 1850. There are varied estimates on the specifications of the *Major Brown,* among them Tilden's, but Chapman's seem to be the most accurate. He was in charge of quartermaster riverboats and was familiar with them.

4 Tilden biographical material is from Brevet Major General George W. Cullum, *Officers and Graduates of the U.S. Military Academy at West Point, N.Y. from Its Establishment in 1802, to 1890 with the Early History of the United States Military Academy* (Cambridge, Mass.: Heritage Press of Houghton, Mifflin and Company, 1891), 2: 46, 47.

5 Bryant P. Tilden, *Notes on the Upper Rio Grande* (Philadelphia: Lindsay and Blakiston, 1847), pp. 9–36. The series of incidents and quotes is in sequence as he describes the river at low water.

6 The survey was apparently made by an engineer with General Wool's army of Chihuahua; Chapman, who had served in that army, probably knew him. That he and his command were well aware of it is plain; references are made continually to distances, sites, and other features that could have come only from a report on the survey.

7 Biographical material on Charles Stillman, Mifflin Kenedy, and Richard King, as well as material on their intertwining relationships, comes from Chauncey Devereux Stillman, *Charles Stillman, 1810–1875* (New York: Chauncey Devereux Stillman, 1950), pp. 3–35; Frank C. Pierce, *A Brief History of the Lower Rio Grande Valley* (Menasha, Wisc.: Collegiate Press of George Banta Publishing Company, 1917), pp. 122, 123. Other sources were Harbert Davenport, "Notes on Early Steamboating on the Rio Grande," *Southwestern Historical Quarterly* (October 1945): 286–89; Marjorie Johnson, "When Steamboats Plied the Rio," *Tip-*

O-Texan (August 1972): 18 – 21; Marilyn McAdams Sibley, "Charles Stillman: A Case Study of Entrepreneurship on the Rio Grande, 1861 – 1865," *Southwestern Historical Quarterly* (April 1973): 229, 230, 239; and the letters to and from Brevet Major Chapman as found in the W. W. Chapman file, Brazos Santiago and Fort Brown files, Kenedy and Company file, Charles Stillman file, and two different files on James B. Armstrong, Quartermaster General Files. Tom Lea, *The King Ranch* (Toronto: Little, Brown & Co., 1957), vol. 1, and Leroy P. Graf, "Economic History of the Lower Rio Grande Valley, 1820 – 1875" (Ph.D. diss., Harvard University, 1940), also have extensive references to the group.

8 Biographical material on W. W. Chapman is from Cullum, *Officers and Graduates*, 1: 667, as well as from the Quartermaster General Files.

9 All letters from, to, or about Brevet Major Chapman are from the W. W. Chapman file, Quartermaster General Files, unless otherwise noted.

10 Scholars have generally held that boats on the Rio Grande were primarily freight vessels with but minimal accommodations for passengers. This is probably true, since the accommodations for passengers, including their victuals, were so outstanding on the *Laurel* that a feature story on her was run in the *American Flag,* October 27, 1847—an issue devoted almost entirely to the taking of Mexico City by General Winfield Scott's army.

11 *American Flag,* May 16, 1849.

12 The official documentation of the *Colonel Cross* lists her as being owned by Richard King and Robert Penny. Penny had been the owner of the *Gazelle,* which he brought to the river during the Mexican War. He stayed on the river after she was lost, apparently investing in several boating ventures. He became a partner in Kenedy and Company.

13 Thomas Baldwin and J. Thomas, *New and Complete Gazeteer of the United States: Full and Complete Review of the Condition, Industry, and Resources of the American Confederacy* (Philadelphia: Lippincott, Grambo and Company, 1854), p. 992. I am indebted to the Francis C. Pray index cards in the Steamship Historical Association of America files for leads to this little-known volume. Mrs. Francis C. Pray also helped in locating the volume at the Public Library of Cincinnati and Hamilton County.

CHAPTER 4

1 Although his name does not appear in any of the many books or articles that
have been written about the Rio Grande, "Robert Penny (deceased)" was listed
as once being a member of the partnership by Stillman, Kenedy, and King in
1855.

2 Copy of a contract to complete the warehouse included in a letter from James B.
Armstrong to Jessup, January 22, 1856. J. B. Armstrong file, Quartermaster General Files. (There are two Armstrong files in these archives: the J. B. Armstrong
file and the James B. Armstrong file. The former is briefer and sketchier.)

3 Chapman's real estate speculations are a matter of record in the Cameron
County clerk's office in Brownsville.

4 Cora Montgomery (Jane McManus Storms Cazneau), *Eagle Pass or Life on the
Border* (Austin: Pemberton Press, 1956; reprint of 1852 ed.), p. 168.

5 Ibid., pp. 177–79.

6 Lieutenant W. T. Smith of the Topographical Engineers made the exploration of
the Rio Grande from El Paso to Fort Leaton during high water in late May and
June 1850. He and Lieutenant Michler were then ordered to survey the river from
Ringgold Barracks to the Presidio del Norte. They began the trip in late August
and went as far upriver as their provisions allowed, some forty miles above the
point reached by Captain Harry Love. That part of the trip from the Salado on
was made on a falling and low river; Smith wrote his reports on the two explorations in January 1851. The reports were accompanied by a cover letter from
Colonel Johnston. All three documents are in the Topographical Engineers File
of the Navy and Old Army Archives, National Archives, Washington, D.C.

7 *Republic*, October 1850; *New York Tribune*, October 5, 1850; *Commercial Adver-
tiser*, October 29, 1850; and *Coast Depot and Shipping Port of the Valley of the
Rio Grande, and the Provinces of Mexico Tributary Thereto, with the Government Map of that Region of Country, Published in 1850, together with The Report of the Explorations of the Rio Grande* (New York: Pudney and Russell, Printers, 1850).

8 *Coast Depot*, pp. 15–23.

9 Colonel M. L. Crimmins, Retired, "Two Thousand Miles by Boat in the Rio
Grande in 1850," *Sul Ross State Teachers College, Bulletin 48*, West Texas Historical and Scientific Association, Number 5, December 1, 1933, p. 45. Colonel

Crimmins edited and reprinted *Coast Depot* in this issue. His introduction contains a brief yet detailed biography of Harry Love, who was apparently properly referred to as Captain John Love. In that biography, he goes into the problems of cost and time involved in supplying El Paso.

10 The estimate of costs is based on extrapolations made from costs of goods to Laredo in a tandem mule train–keelboat operation. More weight was given to mule train costs than to river costs so that expenses would not be underestimated.

11 Chapman to Jessup, August 15, 1851.

12 Kenedy wrote Chapman from Washington on January 12, 1852, restating an offer to buy the *Mentoria* and the *Corvette* made on August 18, 1851. W. W. Chapman file, Quartermaster General Files. At the time he wrote the letter of January 12, Kenedy was aware that the contracts were to be awarded to his company. Jessup had written Chapman on January 5 instructing him to have the contracts concluded and signed, with minor changes suggested by the quartermaster general. See also the letter from Robert B. Kingsbury to Congressman Volney Howard, April 6, 1852, J. B. Armstrong file, Quartermaster General Files.

13 *Report on the Inspection of the Eighth District, Department of Texas, Fort Brown,* Navy and Old Army Archives, National Archives.

14 José María Carvajal was a Texas-born, Kentucky-educated Mexican patriot who helped Texas win her revolution and then went to the aid of Mexico. He took part in the Federalist-Centralist struggles on the river, 1839–41, becoming a loyal leader of the Republic of the Rio Grande. From 1850 to 1853 he led a tariff revolt along the river in protest against government prohibitions and high tariffs, which attracted many Texans and gained the support of Brownsville and Matamoros businessmen. When Matamoros unilaterally reformed national tariffs, his revolt collapsed.

15 This letter and the one cited next are in the J. B. Armstrong file, Quartermaster General Files. It is quite clear from their content that, at the very least, Chapman misinterpreted the facts of competition and steamboats on the Rio Grande to General Jessup. It is also evident that General Jessup was involved in the secrecy and that Mifflin Kenedy was instrumental in Jessup's involvement.

16 Letter, Chapman to General Percival Smith, commandant, Department of Texas, September 7, 1855, J. B. Armstrong file, Quartermaster General Files. Chapman remained with the Eighth Department headquarters in San Antonio until 1855,

when Smith moved them to Corpus Christi. Major Chapman went with headquarters to Corpus Christi, apparently with the understanding that he would be
reassigned to his old post on the Rio Grande. See letter, Robert B. Kingsbury
et al. to Jessup, September 4, 1855, W. W. Chapman file, Quartermaster General
Files. Chapman's biography in Cullum fails to mention his transfer to San
Antonio.

CHAPTER 5

1 For a complete summary of the effects of irrigation on the lower river, see Appendix 2.
2 Armstrong to Jessup, February 25, 1856, James B. Armstrong file, Quartermaster
General Files. Armstrong took over as captain of the *Comanche* in March 1853.
In May he was demoted to clerk, a position he held until mid-January 1855.
3 Armstrong to General Percival F. Smith, February 4, 1856, James B. Armstrong
file, Quartermaster General Files. Armstrong and Chapman had had a disagreement in 1849, and Armstrong had used "strong words" to protect himself. Animosity between them was accepted along the river.
4 Thomas to Garesche, July 12, 1855, James B. Armstrong file, Quartermaster General Files.
5 Jessup to Chapman, March 10, 1855, Letters Sent file, Quartermaster General
Files.
6 Garesche to Jessup, June 15, 1855, James B. Armstrong file, Quartermaster General Files. Unless otherwise noted, all material that follows is from this file, as is
the material dealing with the contract problem. It seems strange that all who
have written about the Rio Grande, directly or indirectly concerned with navigation or with King and Kenedy, have not only ignored the Armstrong case but
have ignored the role of Chapman as well.
7 In W. W. Chapman file, Quartermaster General Files.
8 Mifflin Kenedy file, Quartermaster General Files, and Tom Lea, *The King Ranch*
(Toronto: Little, Brown & Co., 1957), 1: 141. Lea makes it appear that it was Kenedy's first trip to Washington and that the letter was one of introduction to
Jessup. It might have been written as such, if Kenedy had not wished the two
potent Texas politicians to know that he had a relationship with Jessup. Lea

overlooked Kenedy's trip in the winter of 1851/52, when he and Jessup arrived at the initial contract rates. See Chapter 4.

9 Jessup to Gill, June 4, 1856, Letters Sent file, Quartermaster General Files. Strangely, neither this letter nor the one to Chapman of the same day are in the Armstrong files.

10 Lea, *The King Ranch,* 1: 136.

11 Jessup to Cooper, January 16, 1857, Letters Received file, Adjutant General's Office, Navy and Old Army Archives, National Archives, Washington, D.C.

12 Lea, *The King Ranch,* 1: 136, 137. In going through her late husband's papers, Chapman's widow discovered the partnership agreement. After the Civil War, she brought suit to recover. King testified that the document relinquishing claim had been destroyed in the Union occupation of his ranch. The court held for King. Mrs. Chapman died soon after, and King paid her attorney's fees.

13 Armstrong's death is a mystery. There is no death record in the Cameron County clerk's office; he apparently left no will; the inventory of his estate is missing. All that remains of him are the minutes of the Probate Court, beginning in August 1857. Either the estate was never closed out, or the Probate Court minutes are missing. According to the Court of Claims Proceedings, 1856–1860, Judicial, Fiscal, and Social Branch, National Archives, Washington, D.C., he operated his boats past August 1, 1857.

CHAPTER 6

1 Lea covers the entire Armstrong venture and the disposal of his boats in a single paragraph:

Only once was the transportation monopoly held by M. Kenedy & Co. threatened. During the fall of 1855, John Young and Jose San Roman brought the steamers Swan *and* Guadalupe *to the Rio Grande, hoping to skim some of the profit of the trade from* Grampus *and* Comanche. *This competition proved worrisome enough to cause M. Kenedy & Co. to buy it out. In May 1857 Kenedy, King and Stillman paid Young and San Roman a total of $20,000 for the* Swan *and* Guadalupe, *half the sum in promissory notes, the other half consisting of title to one undivided one-eighth interest in all properties and business of M. Kenedy & Co. [Tom Lea,* The King Ranch *(Toronto: Little, Brown & Co., 1957), 1: 74.]*

The handwriting of the period was so bad that Lea might have misread "Nov." for "May." San Román was named executor of Armstrong's estate along with Armstrong's father, William R. Armstrong of Missouri. When the elder Armstrong had to return home, San Román became the sole executor. See *Probate Court Minute Book, 1857-1858,* Brownsville, Cameron County, Texas. John Young was not one of the original members of the group that supported Armstrong. He may have replaced Grogan, who died in 1857, but there is no record of a replacement. His name is never mentioned in any of the records concerning the case or in the James B. Armstrong or J. B. Armstrong files.

Since Armstrong paid but $12,000 for the two boats in 1855, his estate realized a considerable profit. Such high prices paid to various individuals after someone's death have led to various conjectures that I will not treat here. For instance, O'Donnell offered to sell his interest in Kenedy and Company to Armstrong for $8,000, yet after his death in 1855 the partners gave his widow $50,000 for her interest in the company.

2 Senate Report 438, 42d Congress, 3d Sess. (1873). It was noted that Armstrong's heirs had never received their payment because of the Civil War. The recommendation was made that all heirs who had been loyal to the Union divide an amount reduced by Congress to $13,385.09.

3 House Report 659, 43d Congress, 1st Sess. (1874). A special bill to provide relief for Edward S. Armstrong, a Confederate veteran, allowing him to collect his share of the Armstrong claim.

4 Lea, *The King Ranch,* 1: 432, note 8.

5 Letter, Mercurio Martínez, Sr., to George Boyle, March 30, 1964, Mercurio Martínez Collection, Texas A&M University Archives, College Station, Texas; Virgil Lott and Mercurio Martínez, *The Kingdom of Zapata* (San Antonio: Naylor Publishing Co., 1953), pp. 170-71. Both sources refer to the find as a "rudder"; however, Oscar Gutiérrez, who found it, definitely states that it was part of the boat's paddlewheel. "It had many blades, like a windmill," he told me, "but the wood parts were all washed away." Interview, June 11, 1985.

6 This is a story told by almost everyone in Laredo who is familiar with local history. It is undocumented, but its prevalence is such that it must be recognized.

7 John S. "Rip" Ford, *Memoirs,* Barker Texas History Library, University of Texas at Austin, 5: 872-92, presents a summary of this period on the river. See also Lea, *The King Ranch,* 1: 232, 233.

8 As indicated by ship registration and documentation. Judicial, Fiscal, and Social Branch, National Archives, Washington, D.C. Other owners who came to the Rio Grande had documented their vessels elsewhere, making it difficult to identify those in the blockade-busting trade.

9 Lott and Martínez, *The Kingdom of Zapata,* pp. 171, 172.

10 Interview with Fred Hopson of Laredo (March 2, 1985), whose family came to Laredo to help develop the mines. The flatboats are also mentioned in several local histories.

11 All of these boats and others were built at Brownsville immediately following the Civil War. *Enterprise* and *El Primero* were never documented because of the necessity of an oath. They sank during the hurricane of 1867.

12 Frank C. Pierce, *A Brief History of the Lower Rio Grande Valley* (Menasha, Wisc.: Collegiate Press of George Banta Publishing Company, 1917), pp. 56, 57; Lea, *The King Ranch,* 1: 452, note 12.

13 Lea, *The King Ranch,* 1: 452, note 11.

14 George Durham, *Taming the Nueces Strip* (Austin: University of Texas Press, 1962), p. 103.

15 Michael G. Webster, "Intrigue on the Rio Grande: The *Rio Bravo* Affair, 1875," *Southwestern Historical Quarterly* 74:2 (October 1970): 149–64.

16 Biographical information on John Dare Howland is from Doris Ostrander Dawdy, *Artists of the American West: A Biographical Dictionary* (Chicago: Sage Books, 1980), p. 121.

17 *Santa Fe Daily New Mexican,* September 23, 1874.

18 "Alamosa's Steamboat," *Bulletin,* San Luis Valley Historical Society, Inc. 1 (November 1968): 7. Dr. Joe Carter of Adams State College gave me additional information in a personal conversation. The episode is also recounted in Julia Lipsey, *Governor Hunt of Colorado Territory: His Life and Family* (Colorado Springs: J. J. Lipsey, Western Books, 1960), p. 22.

19 Paul Horgan, *Great River: The Rio Grande in North American History* (New York: Holt, Rinehart and Winston, 1971), p. 943. Horgan recounts the way William J. Glasgow, a young lieutenant in 1896, recalled the trip.

20 David P. Pletcher, "Warner P. Sutton and the American-Mexican Trade during the Early Díaz Period," *Southwestern Historical Quarterly* (April 1976): 388.

21 Pierce, *Lower Rio Grande Valley,* p. 126.

22 Interview with Fred Hopson.

23 Biographical information on John Closner is taken from J. Lee Stambaugh and Lillian J. Stambaugh, *The Lower Rio Grande Valley of Texas* (San Antonio: Naylor Publishing Co., 1954), pp. 184–85.

CHAPTER 7

1 Information on the treaties of 1884 and 1889 is taken from quotations of Millard Patterson in the *El Paso Times*, May 3, 1931.
2 Romero to Olney, January 5, 1897, "Correspondence Touching the Negotiation of a Treaty between the United States and Mexico for the Construction of an International Dam in the Rio Grande," *Equitable Distribution of the Waters of the Rio Grande, Proceedings of the International (Water) Boundary Commission, United States and Mexico, Treaties of 1884 and 1889* (Washington, D.C.: Department of State, 1903), 2: 333.
3 From an unidentified El Paso newspaper, Elephant Butte vertical file, Southwest Collection, El Paso Public Library.
4 Maurice G. Kelley, "Water Law in the Rio Grande Valley of Texas as Modified by an International Boundary" (Unpublished ms., 1951), p. 5.
5 "Special Report of the United States Commissioner Covering Joint Report of the Joint Commission on the Bancos known as 'El Banco de Camargo,' 'El Banco de Vela,' 'El Banco de Granjeno,' 'El Banco de Santa Margarita' on the Lower Rio Grande," *Equitable Distribution,* 1: 173–76.
6 "A Study of the Use of Water for Irrigation on the Rio Grande del Norte," *Equitable Distribution,* 2: 284.
7 *Equitable Distribution,* 2: 333–35.
8 *United States* v. *The Rio Grande Dam & Irrigation Co., et al.,* August 24, 1900.
9 Material on the hearings, including the McGowan testimony, is taken from "Testimony Submitted to the Committee on Foreign Affairs for the Distribution of the Waters of the Rio Grande between the United States of America and the United States of Mexico, and for the purpose of Building an International Dam and Reservoir on said river at El Paso, Tex.," *Equitable Distribution,* 2: 371–73.
10 The survey of the river is found in "Proceedings of International (Water) Boundary Commission Measurements of Flow of the Rio Grande and tributaries, with reference to the probable effect on the navigability of the lower river of the pro-

posed obstruction of the flow by the Rio Grande Dam and Irrigation Company," *Equitable Distribution,* 2: 401–25.

11 Virgil Lott and Mercurio Martínez, *The Kingdom of Zapata* (San Antonio: Naylor Publishing Co., 1953), pp. 173–76; J. Lee Stambaugh and Lillian J. Stambaugh, *The Lower Rio Grande Valley of Texas* (San Antonio: Naylor Publishing Co., 1954), pp. 185–87.

12 Martin's complete story can be found in the Elephant Butte vertical file of the Southwest Collection, El Paso Public Library. The newspaper clipping is undated and unidentified. The 1923 date given is an estimate based on the first sentence.

13 The short lives of inland river steamers are well documented. Cf. "Loss List" in William M. Lytle and Forrest R. Holdcamper, *Merchant Steam Vessels of the United States, 1790–1868: The Lytle-Holdcamper List,* ed. C. Bradford Mitchell (Staten Island, N.Y.: Steamship Historical Society of America, Inc., 1975), pp. 238–308.

14 W. W. Follett, "Supplemental Report of the American Consulting Engineer," *Joint Report of the Consulting Engineers on Field Operations of 1910–1911, Proceedings of the International Boundary Commission, United States and Mexico, American Section* (Washington, D.C.: Department of State, 1912), pp. 23–26.

15 Major William H. Emory, *United States and Mexico Boundary Survey made under the Direction of the Secretary of the Interior* (Washington, D.C.: A. O. P. Nicholson, n.d.), pp. 70, 71.

APPENDIX 2

1 All information on which this study is based is found in *Equitable Distribution of the Waters of the Rio Grande, Proceedings of the International (Water) Boundary Commission, United States and Mexico, Treaties of 1884 and 1889* (Washington, D.C.: Department of State, 1903), vol. 2. This particular information is on p. 421.

2 Ibid., p. 418.

3 Ibid., p. 419.

4 Ibid., p. 417.

5 Ibid., p. 300.

6 Ibid., pp. 302–17.

7 Ibid., pp. 317–23.

8 Ibid., p. 300.

9 Ibid., pp. 300, 301, 422–24.

10 San Marcial flow is not given per se in the tables, except for 1900/01. The flow listed is based on the fact that a loss of 14 percent of the San Marcial flow was experienced at El Paso; thus the San Marcial flow could be calculated. In addition, the figure was checked for accuracy by taking the 1901 summer flow and adding in losses of flow due to upriver irrigation.

Selected Bibliography

The following bibliography is intended as a guide for further reading about the history of the Rio Grande and navigation on it and other western rivers. It includes basic material for an understanding of either. However, it does not contain all material referenced in the text.

BOOKS AND ARTICLES

"Alamosa's Steamboat." *Bulletin,* San Luis Valley Historical Society, Inc. 1: 7.

Baldwin, Thomas, and Thomas, J. *Full and Complete Gazeteer of the United States: Full and Complete Review of the Condition, Industry, and Resources of the American Confederacy.* Philadelphia: Lippincott, Grambo and Company, 1854.

Berlandier, Jean Louis. *Journey to Mexico in the Years 1828 to 1834.* Translated by Sheila M. Ohlendorf, Josette M. Bigelow, and Mary M. Standifer. 2 vols. Austin: Texas State Historical Association, 1980.

Brown, John Henry. *History of Texas from 1685 to 1892.* 2 vols. 1892. Reprint. Austin: Jenkins Publishing Company, 1970.

Calleja del Rey, Felix. "Nuevo Santander in 1795: A Provincial Inspection." Translated and edited by David M. Vigness. *Southwestern Historical Quarterly* (April 1972).

Coast Depot and Shipping Port of the Valley of the Rio Grande, and the Provinces of Mexico Tributary Thereto, With an Important Map of That Region of the Country, Together with the Report of the Exploration of the Rio Grande. New York: Pudney and Russell, Printers, 1850.

Cullum, General George W. *Officers and Graduates of the United States Military Academy at New York from Its Establishment in 1802, to 1890, with the Early History of the United States Military Academy.* Boston: Cambridge Press of Houghton, Mifflin and Company, 1891.

Drago, Harry Sinclair. *The Steamboaters: From the Early Side-Wheelers to the Big Packets.* New York: Dodd, Mead and Company, 1967.

Edwards, Charles. *Rio Grande and Texas Land Company.* New York: n.p., 1834.

————. *Texas and Coahuila, with an Exposition of the Latest Colonization Law (28th Day of April, 1832).* New York: Sold by S. Decamp and Company, Wall Street, 1834.

Egerton, William H. *Important Report Just Received from the Government Surveyor for the Tracts of Land Owned by the Rio Grande and Texas Land Co.* New York: Osborn and Buckingham, Printers, 1835.

Equitable Distribution of the Waters of the Rio Grande, Proceedings of the International (Water) Boundary Commission, United States and Mexico, Treaties of 1884 and 1889. 2 vols. Washington, D.C.: Department of State, 1903.

de Escudero, J. A. *Noticias estadísticas del estado de Chihuahua.* Mexico City: En la Oficina del Puente de Palacio y Flamencos num. 1, por Juan Ojeda, 1834.

Estados general de las fundaciónes hechas por Don José Escandón en la colonia del Nuevo Santander, Costa del Seno mexicano, Documentos originales que conténen la inspección de la provincia efectuada por el capitán de dragones Don José Tienda de Cuervo, el informe del mismo al Virrey, y un apéndice con la relación histórica de la colonia del Nuevo Santander, por Fr. Vicente Santa María. 2 vols. Mexico City: Talleres Gráficos de la Nacion, 1930.

Follett, W. W. "Supplemental Report of the American Consulting Engineer." *Joint Report of the Consulting Engineers on Field Operations of 1910–1911. Proceedings of the International Boundary Commission, United States and Mexico, American Section.* Washington, D.C.: Department of State, 1912.

Foster, Helen B. "Steamship Navigation in Pennsylvania." M.A. thesis, Pennsylvania State College, 1933.

García Purón, Manuel. *México y sus gobernantes.* 2d ed. Mexico City: Librería de Porrúa, S.A., 1964.

Graf, Leroy P. "Economic History of the Lower Rio Grande Valley 1820–1875." Ph.D. diss., Harvard University, 1940.

Green, Thomas Jefferson. *Journal of the Texian Expedition against Mier, Subsequent Imprisonment of the Author, His Sufferings and Final Escape from the Castle Perote, with Reflections upon the Present Political and Probable Future Relations of Texas, Mexico, and the United States.* 1844. Reprint. Austin: Steck Company, 1935.

Haney, P. L. "The International Controversy over the Waters of the Upper Rio Grande." M.A. thesis, Texas Western College, 1948.

Henson, Margaret Swett. *Juan Davis Bradburn*. College Station: Texas A&M University Press, 1982.

Horgan, Paul. *Great River: The Rio Grande in North American History*. New York: Rinehart and Winston, 1954.

Hunter, Louis. *Steamboats on the Western Rivers*. Cambridge, Mass.: Harvard University Press, 1949.

Inventory of County Archives of Texas, No. 240, Webb County (Laredo). N.p.: Works Progress Administration, 1938.

Kennedy, William. *The Rise, Progress, and Prospects of the Republic of Texas*. 2d ed., 1841. Reprint. Fort Worth: Molyneaux Craftsmen, 1923.

Lea, Tom. *The King Ranch*. 2 vols. Toronto: Little, Brown & Co., 1957.

Lipsey, Julia. *Governor Hunt of Colorado Territory: His Life and Family*. Colorado Springs: J. J. Lipsey, Western Books, 1960.

Lott, Virgil E., and Martínez, Mercurio. *Kingdom of Zapata*. San Antonio: Naylor Publishing Company, 1953.

Lytle, William M., and Holdcamper, Forrest R. *Merchant Steam Vessels of the United States, 1790–1868: The Lytle-Holdcamper List*. Edited by C. Bradford Mitchell. Staten Island, N.Y.: Steamship Historical Society of America, Inc., 1975.

Montgomery, Cora (Jane McManus Storms Cazneau). *Eagle Pass or Life on the Border*. 1852. Reprint. Austin: Pemberton Press, 1956.

Nance, Joseph Milton. *Texas After San Jacinto: The Texas-Mexican Frontier 1836–1841*. Austin: University of Texas Press, 1963.

Ortiz y Ayala, Teodoro. *Resumen de la estadística del imperio mexicano*. Edited by Tarsicio García Díaz. Mexico City: Universadad Nacional Autónoma de México, 1968.

Pierce, Frank C. *A Brief History of the Lower Rio Grande Valley*. Menasha, Wisc.: Collegiate Press of George Banta Publishing Company, 1917.

Prieto, Alejandro. *Historia, geografica, y estadística de Tamaulipas*. 1873. Reprint. Mexico City: Manuel Porrus, Librio, 1949.

Secretario de Despacho del Estado de Chihuahua. *Memoria sobre la administración pública del estado, Leyda al honorable congreso, Tercero constitucional, en 4 de julio 1831*. Mexico City: Imprenta Gobierno, a Cargo C. Sabino Cano, 1831.

Sibley, Marilyn McAdams. "Charles Stillman: A Case Study of Entrepreneurship on the Rio Grande, 1861–1865." *Southwestern Historical Quarterly* (April 1973).

Stillman, Chauncey Devereux. *Charles Stillman, 1810–1875.* New York: Chauncey Devereux Stillman, 1950.

Thompson, Jerry. *Sabers on the Rio Grande.* Austin: Presidial Press, 1974.

Tilden, Bryant P. *Notes on the Upper Rio Grande.* Philadelphia: Lindsay and Blakiston, 1847.

ARCHIVES

National Archives, Washington, D.C.

Navy and Old Army Archives

Armstrong, J. B. File. Quartermaster General's Office. Consolidated File, Group 92.

Armstrong, James B. File. Quartermaster General's Office. Consolidated File, Group 92.

Chapman, W. W. File. Quartermaster General's Office. Consolidated File, Group 92.

Kenedy, Mifflin. File. Quartermaster General's Office. Consolidated File, Group 92.

Letters Received. File. Adjutant General's Office. Correspondence.

Letters Received. File. Quartermaster General's Office. Consolidated File, Group 92.

Letters Sent. File. Adjutant General's Office. Correspondence.

Letters Sent. File. Quartermaster General's Office. Consolidated File, Group 92.

Stillman, Charles. File. Quartermaster General's Office. Consolidated File, Group 92.

Judicial, Fiscal, and Social Branch

Documentation and Registry. United States Merchant Ships.

Court of Claims. Proceedings. 1856–1860.

Index